MONTPARNASSE

MONTPARNASSE

Paris's District of
Memory and Desire

John Baxter

HARPER PERENNIAL

NEW YORK • LONDON • TORONTO • SYDNEY • NEW DELHI • AUCKLAND

HarperCollins books may be purchased for educational, business, or sales promotional use. For information, please email the Special Markets Department at SPsales@harpercollins.com.

FIRST EDITION

Designed by Jamie Kerner

Map by Tony Foster

Library of Congress Cataloging-in-Publication Data has been applied for.

ISBN 978-0-06-267904-8

17 18 19 20 21   LSC   10 9 8 7 6 5 4 3 2 1

For my French family, who took me in.
What gift could be greater than that?

From the shores
of oval oceans
in the oxidized Orient
Onyx-eyed Odalisques
and ornithologists
observe
the flight
of Eros obsolete
And "Immortality"
mildews . . .
in the museums of the moon.

Mina Loy, from "Lunar Baedeker," 1923

Contents

Map		*xiii*
Introduction: On the Beach		*xvii*
1	FOUR CAFÉS, ONE QUARTER	1
2	THE WALLED CITY	14
3	WE'LL ALWAYS HAVE MONTPARNASSE	24
4	HIRED HELP	37
5	THE OTHER BOHEMIANS	47
6	SVENGALI	61
7	ABSINTHE AND ALCHEMY: CLOSERIE DES LILAS	72
8	A ROOM WITH A VIEW	82
9	WOMEN AND MAN: THE LOVE LIFE OF MAN RAY	91
10	THE QUEEN OF MONTPARNASSE	102

11 MAD, BAD, AND DANGEROUS TO KNOW   109

12 CLOSE TO THE BULL:
    DONALD OGDEN STEWART   119

13 A WIT ON THE BLACK LIST:
    MEETING DONALD OGDEN STEWART   128

14 *LE DANCING*   132

15 THE SOUND OF ONE HAND READING   143

16 A DEPOT NAMED DESIRE   154

17 THE FIFTH-BEST TARTARE IN PARIS   165

18 MARTHE RICHARD: SPYING FRENCH-STYLE   179

19 LE SÉLECT: A HORIZONTAL TOWER OF BABEL 191

20 CIMETIÈRE DU MONTPARNASSE   200

21 THE BEST NIGHTCLUB THAT EVER WAS   214

Acknowledgments   225
Photographic and Illustration Credits   227
Index   229

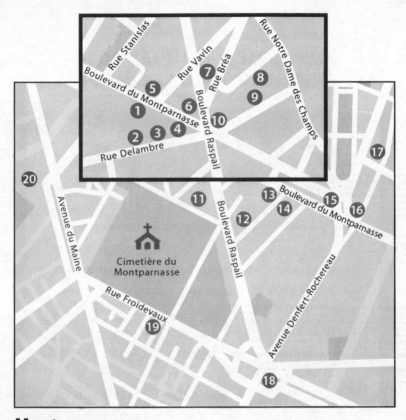

Montparnasse

1   La Coupole
2   Dingo Bar
3   At the Sign of the Black Manikin
4   Café du Dôme
5   Le Sélect
6   La Rotonde
7   Café Charivari
8   Académie Carmen
9   Académie Colarossi
10 Model Market
11 Le Sphinx
12 Man Ray Home
13 Le Jockey
14 Café Rosalie & the Cité des Artistes
15 Closerie des Lilas and Ney Statue
16 Bal Bullier
17 Man Ray Studio
18 Catacombs and Ledoux
    Customs Houses and La Californie
19 Hemingway Studio,
    69 rue Froidevaux
20 Gare Montparnasse

MONTPARNASSE

ON THE BEACH

We have lingered in the chambers of the sea
By sea-girls wreathed with seaweed red and brown
Till human voices wake us, and we drown.

T. S. ELIOT, FROM "THE LOVE SONG OF
J. ALFRED PRUFROCK"

On winter mornings, the cafés of Montparnasse exude a chill, like sea caves at low tide.

Waiting for the rain to ease and dawdling over a *café crème* already gone cold, I enjoyed the faintly echoing emptiness of the largest of them, La Coupole.

A lone waiter glided by, glanced at my cup, and, fish-like, idled away among the square pillars that, as precisely as the measures of an alexandrine, parse the lofty space under the cupola that gives the café its name. From the kitchen, a distant clank hinted at food in preparation, but not much, and not soon.

At the grand opening of La Coupole on December 20, 1927, 2,500 guests affirmed a Montparnasse tradition by draining 1,200 bottles of champagne. Unless you count the Folies Bergère's newest star, Josephine Baker, few Americans were present, a situation decisively reversed in the decade that followed. Every liner from New York brought hordes of new arrivals flooding into La Coupole. Those who didn't find seats at the mirrored cocktail bar took tables in one of its two restaurants, or headed downstairs to its dance hall, perhaps also visiting the marbled art deco restrooms, amenities so chic it still feels vulgar to do anything more physical there than wash one's hands.

Its slick decor gives no hint that La Coupole started

La Coupole in the 1920s.

life as a coal and firewood depot, a not uncommon genesis for Paris cafés, some of which developed from impromptu canteens where haulers took a break and a hot drink between deliveries. In 1926, the Juglar yard at 102 Boulevard du Montparnasse came on the market just as Ernest Fraux and his brother-in-law René Lafon resigned as managers of the nearby Café du Dôme.

Swelling numbers of American tourists had convinced them there was room for a café built with foreigners in mind. Buying the coal yard cheap, they constructed an entertainment center providing food, drink, and diversion eighteen hours a day. Locals shunned this "giant cabaret on the German model" but Americans were enthusiastic. Arriving mid-afternoon for the daily tea dance, they could share martinis and cosmopolitans with friends at the cocktail hour, enjoy a long dinner, then tango or fox-trot into the early hours.

As oblivious to what went on outside as they had been on the Cunard or White Star liners that carried them across the Atlantic, clients of the Coupole were often startled, emerging at four in the morning in search of a cab, to find, standing by the door, the same pale girl with her tray of posies and toys who'd been there when they entered twelve hours before. Beyond her shuffled the sleepless parade of panhandlers and prostitutes, street musicians, jugglers, miscellaneous bohemians, and practitioners of the three-card trick who cruised the boulevard from dusk to dawn.

Some visitors looked away, embarrassed by this display of shabbiness and need. Others sensed in its presence an implied rebuke. Scott Fitzgerald, his way barred by a street vendor not unlike the girl at La Coupole, sent her tray flying. Another tourist, noticing for the first time the handful of notes and coins he'd been given in change, scattered it impulsively on the sidewalk among the smeared spit and cigarette butts. "There's your cheap franc," he murmured to a companion as men and women scrambled for the money. "Not worth the trouble of putting it in your pocket."

Amedeo Modigliani, Pablo Picasso, and André Salmon, 1916.

THE PILLARS OF LA COUPOLE

As La Coupole neared completion in 1927, the management asked art experts Charles Dufresne, Florent Fels, and André Salmon to propose painters to decorate its sixteen pillars and seventeen half pillars or pilasters.

Officially, they chose "artists faithful to the bohemian spirit of Montparnasse," but for Salmon to have approached, for example, his good friend Pablo

Picasso would have been insulting. Most of those selected were relative unknowns, dismissed, unkindly, by one critic as "Russians, Poles, and Danubians [who] reflect the nature of Montparnasse in general as a refuge for exiles and outlaws." Between twenty-eight and thirty artists were involved. (Two pilasters can't be attributed, three or four other attributions are speculative, and two damaged columns were repainted during renovations in 1987.) It was long believed the management paid for the work in free meals, but, from accounts discovered in 1993, we now know that some shrewd accountant, estimating the cost of providing thirty hungry painters with dinners in perpetuity, opted for payment in cash. He allocated FF23,000: about $25,000 today. Given these modest rates, it's not surprising only a few paintings rise above the decorative. They include the most frequently reproduced image, of an African in a top hat and monocle with his date passed out in his lap. Sometimes misattributed to Fernand Léger, it's actually by Marie Vassilieff, best known for her dolls and marionettes. Jules Pascin can be seen on another column, seated, in his trademark bowler hat. Victor Robiquet immortalized Josephine Baker, plumed in ostrich feathers, and Vassilieff showed writer George Duhamel playing the flute, as he'd done to amuse himself in the trenches of the Somme. ("I'd have preferred a piano," he said, "but I couldn't get one into my pack.")

In almost a century, La Coupole has undergone many changes. The dance hall survives, but at the expense of the first-floor restaurant and a roof-top terrace where the rowdier elements of Montparnasse sometimes played bicycle polo. Both were absorbed into the additional levels of office space added by the current owners. However, the 600-seat brasserie, now designated a national monument, remains, along with its pillars, mostly intact.

Pilaster by Marie Vassilieff.

FOUR CAFÉS, ONE QUARTER

Great artists have no country.
ALFRED DE MUSSET

Le Sélect, the Café du Dôme, La Rotonde, and La Coupole made up the foundations of what expatriates came to call "the quarter." For almost a century, the four competed with one another, each enjoying a few vintage seasons as *the* place to see and be seen: for one golden moment what the Greeks called "the navel of the world." (At the time of writing, the title belonged to the Rotonde, after President Emmanuel Macron took it over for a night to celebrate his 2017 victory at the polls.)

Most of what today's visitors know of Montparnasse between the wars comes from Ernest Hemingway's *A Moveable Feast*, but it takes nothing away from the charm of that book to acknowledge it is far from the whole story. Distance, in lending enchantment, exacts a high price in accuracy. Hemingway's nostalgia for Paris was an affliction of ill health and old age. During the seven years he lived there, he criticized harshly both Montparnasse and his fellow expatriates. At one particularly low point, he dismissed the district as "more a state of mind than a geographical area. This state of mind is principally contempt." With a hint of his later tendency to pontificate, he continued, "Those who work have the greatest contempt for those who don't. The loafers are leading their own lives and it is bad form to mention work. Young painters have contempt for old painters, and that works both ways too. There are contemptuous critics and contemptuous writers. Everybody seems to dislike everybody else."

Some of the prevailing prejudice was racial. In 1914, surveying the polyglot clientele of the Rotonde, poet Guillaume Apollinaire, himself a Pole, saw it in terms of national divisions. "On one side are the Germans. Opposite are the Slavs. The Jews are indifferent, and sit where they like." Africans and African-Americans were frequently stigmatized. In 1928, a café owner explained the scarcity of aristocratic visitors. "Blue bloods?" he said. "We are chiefly intrigued by *black* blood; negro painting, negro sculpture, negro music, and negro dancing." Canadian writer Morley Callaghan blamed the failure of his Jewish friend Edward

Titus to be embraced by the Montparnos, as long-time ex-pats liked to call themselves, on the fact that "there was a lot of anti-Semitism in the quarter." Even Hemingway can't be absolved of that particular bigotry. Writing to John Dos Passos in 1924, he voiced a concern that his book *in our time* would be bought by the Jewish firm of Boni & Liveright. "I'm all for keeping it out of the manuals of the Semites as long as possible."

Resentments among the Montparnos were most virulent where wealth and poverty clashed. "There were hundreds of men and women who had only the café as a resting place," wrote novelist Michel Georges-Michel, "and here they were confronted by the more fortunate; Swedish girls with emerald earrings; American girls who had champagne and mussels or onion soup in the inner room; models, even, who were sometimes paid for posing and who then sipped liqueurs and looked down on female artists."

Less successful expatriates accepted such social and racial tensions as the price of enjoying what cafés provided. To anyone living in a bug-infested rooming house without heat or running water, their warmth, the easy companion-ship of the zinc, as the bar was called, and such fragments of domesticity as the newspapers provided for regulars and the pigeonholes at the rear of some cafés in which they could keep their napkins between meals were the nearest thing to a home. Decades later, when he'd forgotten much else, these details are what Hemingway remembered. In 1960, his memory jogged by a query from Lillian Ross as to what he would do should he revisit Paris, he told her gruffly, "Want to go to cafés where I know no one but one waiter and his replacement, see all the new pictures and the old ones, go to the bike races and the fights, and see the new riders and fighters. Find good, cheap restaurants where you can keep your own napkin."

With private telephones rare and people often moving at short notice, leaving no forwarding address, certain cafés also served as gathering places for those with shared interests or professions. Musicians, theater extras, operatic choristers, artists' models, prostitutes: all congregated in specific cafés where potential employers could find them. Friends even wrote to them there, or left notes. Jacqueline Goddard, one of Man Ray's models, was nostalgic for that intimacy. "We went to the bar of La Coupole," she said. "Bob, the barman, was a terribly nice chap. As there was no telephone in those days, everybody used him to leave messages. At the Dôme, we also had a little place behind the door for letters." She sighed. "The telephone was the death of Montparnasse."

Until the Sélect and Coupole opened, in 1923 and 1927, respectively, life in Montparnasse revolved around the Dôme and Rotonde. The latter opened in 1910 as a canteen for students from the art schools of rue de la Grande-Chaumière, the owner sometimes accepting canvases in exchange for food. Russians colonized it after the 1917 revolution, to be supplanted in 1920 by tourists from America. In March 1922, after barely four months in Paris but already seeing himself as a Montparno, Ernest Hemingway complained on their behalf that "the scum of Greenwich Village, New York, has been skimmed off and deposited in large ladles on that section of Paris adjacent to the Café Rotonde. New scum, of course, has risen to take the place of the old, but the oldest scum, the thickest scum and the scummiest scum has come across the ocean, somehow, and with its afternoon and evening levees has made the Rotonde the leading Latin Quarter showplace for tourists in search of atmosphere. A first look into the smoky, high-ceilinged, table-crammed interior of the Rotonde gives the same feeling that hits you as you step into the bird house at the zoo."

As a newcomer, Ernest could be forgiven for wrongly including Montparnasse in the Latin Quarter. As the American restaurant critic Julian Street admonished in 1929, "the Montparnasse district, still largely inhabited by artists, writers, students, and loafers, is *not* the Latin Quarter, as it is sometimes called, the latter being the region surrounding the Sorbonne, at the other side of the Luxembourg gardens."

The Montparnos didn't see Montparnasse as a quarter at all, in the sense of "native quarter" or "diplomatic quarter," but rather as *the* quarter, a zone so specific and distinctive as to need no defining adjective. Did one speak of "the *tropical* equator" or "the *Arctic* North Pole"? Further to signify its status sui generis, locals, with calculated cool, always spelled "quarter" with a lowercase *q*—something Hemingway had learned by the time he wrote in his poem "Montparnasse" that "there are never any suicides in the quarter among people one knows," omitting the capital letter like the weariest boulevardier.

After Spaniards took over the Rotonde, colonizing its ground floor with a *peña* or discussion group each afternoon, under the chairmanship of the ranking Hispanic intellectual, the café doubled in size, expanding along Boulevard du Montparnasse. During renovations, its American clientele migrated across the boulevard to the Café du Dôme. Those who'd joked that a cabbie stuck with a Yank too drunk to remember his hotel simply dumped him at the Rotonde now said the same about the Dôme.

Unable to accommodate all the new arrivals, the Dôme installed further tables and chairs on the sidewalk to create what was called the terrace. As such space had to be rented from the city, terrace prices were higher, but with the franc at 30 to the dollar and a four-course meal, with wine, costing the equivalent of 18 cents, who any longer even bothered to look at the bill? "And we sit outside the Dôme Café," Hemingway wrote to Sherwood Anderson, "opposite the Rotonde that's being redecorated, warmed up against one of those charcoal brazziers and it's so damned cold outside and the brazzier makes it so warm and we drink rum punch, hot, and the rhum enters into us like the Holy Spirit."

Their corner locations made both the Rotonde and the Dôme ideal for freeloaders. Stationed on the terrace of the Dôme, Henry Miller dawdled through his afternoons, alert for some passing acquaintance who would buy him

Terrace at the Dôme, with charcoal braziers. (Georges Leroux)

the next drink but also pay for the pile of saucers on his table, each one representing a beverage already consumed. Others, somberly dressed, loitered there until a funeral passed, headed for the nearby cemetery. With no idea who was being buried, they joined the procession walking behind the coffin, since it was customary for the family, after the interment, to offer mourners a supper.

Literature didn't flourish in this fragmented culture. "Paris is a very difficult place to work unless he is dull and serious," said Montreal-born poet and memoirist John Glassco. Nobody came to the Dôme or Rotonde to write, but rather to avoid writing. Hemingway, unable to work in the two-room apartment he shared with his wife and child on rue du Cardinal-Lemoine, found peace and quiet in the Closerie des Lilas, a kilometer away from the rowdier watering holes.

Expatriate life had a way of sapping creativity. In Robert Sherwood's play *The Petrified Forest*, failed novelist Alan Squier, who has run off to France with his publisher's wife, evokes the lassitude that reduced many writers to torpor. "She was very liberal to me. She saw in me a major artist, profound but inarticulate. She thought that all I needed was background, so she proceeded to give it to me—with southern exposure and a fine view of the Mediterranean. For eight years I reclined there on the

Riviera, on my background. I waited for the major artist to emerge and say something of enduring importance. But he preferred to remain inarticulate."

Mostly, Montparnasse and the cafés produced jottings, epigrams, and anecdotes, an uncomfortable fact articulated by the critic H. L. Mencken when he dismissed Hemingway's *in our time* as "sketches in the bold, bad manner of the Café du Dôme."

Not that such shards didn't occasionally achieve greatness. As I sat in La Coupole that winter morning, I could see the façade of Le Sélect, intermittently visible through veils of rain. In the ocean that was Montparnasse, that had been its Sargasso Sea, a swirl of social debris: addicts, whores, thieves, the homeless, the desperate, prowled by the sharks that preyed on them. There, American poet Hart Crane paused in brawling drunkenly with its waiters to pen an elegy to the greatest of maritime writers, Herman Melville.

> *Often beneath the wave, wide from this ledge*
> *The dice of drowned men's bones he saw bequeath*
> *An embassy. . . .*

In 1932, rescued from the Santé prison after the last fracas and shipped back to New York to dry out, Crane veered south to Cuba instead and, on the return voyage, slaked his thirst for oblivion by leaping into the Caribbean, his body never found.

> . . . —*sleep, death, desire,*
> *Close round one instant in one floating flower.*

Poetry like Crane's had lured me to Paris. Turning my back on an authentic tropical coast of sea and sand, I'd crossed the world to embrace a culture of artificial beaches and symbolic oceans where the most important of its literary magazines was called, appropriately, *transition*—a title that, like "quarter," eschewed the capital. That I was in good company—Hemingway, Fitzgerald, Miller, Man Ray, Dalí, Trotsky, Lenin, Crane—didn't make the apostasy any less strange.

The high tide of Montparnasse was brief, from 1920 to 1935. Since their work sold mainly outside France, expatriate writers and publishers suffered less in the stock market crash of 1929 than the restaurateurs and shopkeepers who served them, but as the Depression eroded even "old money," exiles whose wealth had freed them to escape early to Paris became the first to leave. Those accustomed to living by their wits stayed on, at least as long as magazines and newspapers wanted news of the city. Not until the mid-1930s, amid a general feeling of "the parade's gone by" as far as France was concerned, did they drift back to New York, London, and Madrid.

For half a generation, each evening had brought more castaways to this reef, foaming phosphorescent at the end of civilization's night. Most lingered only for a season in the tidal pools of its cafés, mesmerized by the debutantes and whores, gigolos and wastrels who scuttled and squirmed around them, gaudy as sea anemones, spasmodic as mating grunion on a California beach. Why did these people come here? Why did they stay? Who knew? But then, what reason, other than the volatility of this society, did they need? As one giddy visitor murmured in 1929, "My dear, at first I was uncertain whether the Dôme was a place or a state of mind or a disease. It is all three!" Ebb and flow, ebb and flow . . . Montparnasse, like the sea, was an environment where nothing remained long in one place. As the title of one memoir observed, it was, above all, a *moveable* feast. But for the expatriates who lingered here a season or two, its transitoriness was lure enough.

WHY "MONTPARNASSE"?

1st Actor: Gods of the theater, smile on us.
2nd Actor: You who sit up there stern in judgment,
  smile on us.
1st Actor: You who look down on actors ...
Both (aside): And who doesn't?
Bless this yearly festival and smile on us.

  Stephen Sondheim, *The Frogs* (after Aristophanes)

Traditionally, Apollo and the nine goddesses known
as the Muses make their home on the mountain in
Greece called Parnassus. Believed to inspire creativity, they are Calliope (epic poetry), Clio (history),
Euterpe (lyric poetry), Thalia (comedy and pastoral
poetry), Melpomene (tragedy), Terpsichore (dance),
Erato (love poetry), Polyhymnia (sacred poetry), and
Urania (astronomy). Exclusively deities of performance, their blessing was solicited before any play
or public recitation. (There were no Muses for
sculptors, painters, and architects, regarded in
Attic Greece as mere workmen, too lowly for divine
patronage.)

    During the eighteenth century, students from
the religious schools of the Latin Quarter, panting

up this hill at the southern limit of Paris, may have looked back at the city spreading along the banks of the Seine and thought themselves masters of the known world. Through the haze of wine purchased from the locals, this unpromising landfill, formed from the rubble of urban expansion and fertilized by the corpses of the nameless dead, could have felt like their own Parnassus, an illusion they celebrated by reciting or improvising verse.

Still then nameless, the hill first appeared on a map, the *Lutetia Parisiorum vulgo* of Johannes Janssonius, in 1657, which identified the track leading to its summit as the Chemin d'Enfer: the Road to Hell. The district looked doomed to remain a wasteland until, in 1667, Louis XIV chose to build an observatory there. (Charles II of England, envious, immediately commissioned his own for Greenwich.) Sometime during the next fifty years, it became officially Montparnasse, since in 1725 the city annexed it under that name. A road was laid along the ridge. Tunneling below the unstable topsoil, quarrymen mined the fine-grained limestone from which a greater Paris would be built, and where soon the Muses, though far from home, would again be heard.

THE WALLED CITY

Admiror, O paries, te non cecidisse, qui tot
scriptorium taedia sustineas. *(Colloquially
translated as "I wonder that this wall don't split
/ From being stuck with all this shit.")*
GRAFFITO ON THE WALLS OF
HERCULANEUM, AD 79

WITH EACH EXPANSION OF PARIS, ITS OLD WALLS WERE
demolished and new ones built. By the eighteenth century, they enclosed Montparnasse, and travelers from the
south found their way barred by the Wall of the Farmers
General. (The Passage d'Enfer—Hell's Alley—a cobbled
lane behind 31 and 31 bis rue Campagne-Premiere, marks
its former position.) The buildings of rue Daguerre have
long since absorbed its stones, but Claude Nicolas Le-

doux's customs houses, dating from 1785, survive on Place Denfert-Rochereau, at the eastern end of the ridge, one of them doubling as the entrance to the ossuary known as the Catacombs.

Gates in the wall funneled visitors past customs officers or *douaniers* who extracted a duty on goods intended for sale. They were particularly on the alert for salt, so rare that the tax on it, known as *la gabelle*, generated 6 percent of France's national income. Smugglers, often women, hid salt under their skirts. The protests (or giggles) as inspectors searched for contraband added to the ribald character of life in the area just outside the walls that Parisians would come to call *le ẓone*. Not immune to this casual morality, some customs officers left the service to open food or wine shops. One nineteenth-century official, Henri Rousseau, known as "Le Douanier," became an artist, painting his mysterious naive canvases only on Sundays, his one day off.

Merchants arriving at the wall often loitered outside for a day or two. Some avoided city taxes by selling their goods there: the first duty-free outlets. Others rested, cleaning up before experiencing the wonders of Paris. To accommodate them, sellers of refreshments, entertainment, and sex opened inns, brothels, and food shops, the most famous named for that fantastic and imaginary land, California.

Along with the first recorded slur on Paris coffee, a description of 1859 gave La Californie the kind of review every restaurateur dreads.

> *Next to some houses of unhealthy appearance you will find a muddy alley where are installed some sellers of hot water, black in color, for a sou a cup. This is the Bar of Smelly Feet. Move on! At the end of the mud is La Californie. It's flanked by two courtyards, in one of which you will see some wormy tables where patrons can sit in good weather. The other is for people who need to throw up before they go in search of the whores on Avenue du Maine.*
>
> *The principal ground floor dining room is immense. To reach it, you pass through the kitchen, supervised from her throne by Madame Cadet, wife of the proprietor. Every day, La Californie serves 5000 portions of beef, veal and mutton. Eight casks of wine are needed to wash them down. Each year, it consumes a thousand sacks of beans, 55 casks of vinegar and 55 of oil, the composition of which has nothing to do with olives.*

Some eating places metamorphosed into dance halls, known as *bals musette*, with music supplied by the *musette de cour*, a kind of bagpipe native to the mountainous Auvergne, traditional home of restaurateurs. Others became *bals jardins*: gardens where patrons could dine, dance, or exploit the privacy of hedges and shrubbery to pursue their amours, either with their lovers or one of the professional ladies who cruised the darker corners. These places took their inspiration from the Parc aux Cerfs or Deer Park kept by Louis XV on the grounds of his palace at Versailles. The woods of what was officially a hunting preserve actually hid a mansion where young courtesans lived, literally awaiting the king's pleasure, under the supervision of his chief

La Californie.

mistress, Madame de Pompadour, who convoyed them secretly to his apartments.

By 1836, Paris boasted 180 permanent *bals musette* and *bals jardins*. Most held balls to celebrate holidays or festivals, particular Mardi Gras, the "Fat Tuesday" in February that inaugurates the fasting of Lent. In 1836, on Mardi Gras alone, carousers could choose from 850 events. Many attended in costume. Others, in a tip of the hat to Louis XV and his Deer Park, wore masks, even if just a simple domino, covering only the eyes.

Other European capitals had pleasure gardens—Tivoli in Copenhagen, the Prater in Vienna, Vauxhall and Sadler's Wells in London—but none to compare with those of Paris. Like today's discos, they competed to offer the loudest bands and most spectacular shows. In 1844, Prefect of Police Gabriel Delessert bowed to public pressure and banned the playing outdoors of "bass drums, snare drums, kettledrums, cymbals, bells, hunting horns, smoke bombs, firearms and artillery pieces." A noisy orchestra, he claimed, "overexcites the dancers and pushes them into disorder and at the same time disturbs the neighbors' sleep."

The Bal de la Grande-Chaumière bragged "it was here that the *chahut* and cancan were invented." A *chahut* or uproar took place when spectators burst onto the floor among dancers, whooping and showing off with high kicks and other acrobatics. Other *bals* hotly disputed the claim. The Moulin Rouge in Montmartre made the strongest case. At one time a bawdy *café-concert*, featuring rude comics and such specialty acts as fart virtuoso Le Pétomane, who could play operatic arias through his anus, it was transformed when prostitutes from its basement dance hall, hoping to stir up some business, erupted among the all-male clientele, raising their skirts to flash bare thighs. Resourcefully, the management hired sixteen of them, and drilled them to high-kick in unison, with much shouting and flourishing of petticoats. Led by such stars as Louise Weber, alias La Goulue (The Glutton), the cancan became a Montmartre institution.

Public dance halls faded away during the late nineteenth century but some still survived when the first expatriates arrived in the 1920s. Novelist Ford Madox Ford, after having his home trashed once too often during rowdy parties, took to renting a *bal musette* for the night. Ernest and Hadley Hemingway often danced in the same place, the Bal de Printemps, since it occupied the ground floor of their apartment building on rue du Cardinal-Lemoine. By then, the orchestras of the old days had dwindled to a lone accordion player. "There were long benches," Hemingway wrote in *The Sun Also Rises*, "and tables ran across the room, and at the far end a dancing-floor. The proprietor got up on a high stool beside the dancing-floor and began to play the accordion. He had a string of bells around one of his ankles and beat time with his foot as he played. Everyone danced. It was hot and we came off the floor perspiring."

A chahut *at the Bal Bullier.*

THE DANCE HALL OF *LES MISÉRABLES*, THE BAL DE LA GRANDE-CHAUMIÈRE

CORNER OF BOULEVARD DE LA GRANDE-CHAUMIÈRE AND RUE BRÉA

By opening the *bal jardin* known as La Grande-Chaumière (The Big Thatched Cottage) in 1783, a Briton named Tickson marked Montparnasse for all time as a community of outsiders. His open-sided garden bar with a straw roof grew into a building of two stories, housing a restaurant and a band for dancing.

During the antimonarchic insurrection of 1832, celebrated by Victor Hugo in *Les Misérables*, the streets of Paris were thronged with military men. To attract them, Tickson added a pistol range and experimented with an early form of the singing commercial. It urged *"Dansez, buvez, prenez un pot de bière, / Buvez un coup. / Le vent qui vient de la Grande-Chaumière / Vous rendra fou"* (Dance, drink, take a pot of beer, / Drink a cup. / The wind that blows from the Grande-Chaumière / Will drive you mad).

Once life in the city settled down, a new owner,

Benoît Fillard, targeted a younger crowd, promising "something for everyone. There are shady avenues, specially constructed for reflection and the expression of tender feelings. There are groves of sycamores and hazelnut trees, ideal for assignations." After young men and their squealing girlfriends had slid down the four-story Montagnes Suisses (Swiss Mountains), they found a square of asphalt, strewn with sand and surrounded by orange trees, and a band playing for dancing. A new promotional jingle linking the park to the latest dance crazes could have served to advertise Paris itself, poised to enter the decades of creativity and style known as *la belle époque*. "*Messieurs les étudiants / Montez à la Chaumière / Pour y danser l'cancan / Et la Robert Macaire. / Toujours toujours toujours / Triomphe des amours*" (Gentleman students, / Climb to the Chaumière / To dance the cancan / And the Robert Macaire. / Always always always / Love conquers all).

Bal de la Grande-Chaumière.

❋ · 3 · ❋

WE'LL ALWAYS HAVE
MONTPARNASSE

Major Strasser: Are you one of those people who
cannot imagine the Germans in their beloved Paris?
Rick: It's not particularly my *beloved Paris.*
CASABLANCA, SCREENPLAY BY JULIUS J. AND
PHILIP G. EPSTEIN AND HOWARD KOCH

THE 1942 FILM *Casablanca* PRESERVES A CLASSIC VIEW OF
exile life: a conglomerate colony, isolated on a foreign
shore, some members desperate to leave, others glad of its
anonymity. By day, oblivious of the locals, they indulge
in aimless diversion. By night, they congregate in cafés
and clubs to pursue doomed love affairs, and to gossip and
intrigue.

Since real life so often imitates bad fiction, it should be
no surprise that Paris between the wars resembled Holly-

wood's French Morocco, particularly in its mix of nationalities: among the principal players, of Swedish, Austrian, British, German, French, and Russian extraction, only Humphrey Bogart was American-born.

In common with Rick Blaine, Ilsa Lund, and Victor Laszlo, the first expatriates drifting to France after World War I generally did so for reasons that had little to do with art or literature. Many were responding to the postwar plunge in the value of the French franc, making Paris one of the cheapest cities in Europe. Still more fled the repressive social and intellectual climate of the United States that culminated in the 1920 Volstead Act and Prohibition. Others simply wanted an excuse to behave badly. Alcohol was cheap and freely available in Paris, as were opium, cannabis, morphine, and cocaine. The French also countenanced most variations of sexual behavior, and tolerated, in Hemingway's phrase, "ladies of all sexes."

Some new arrivals, generally younger and poorer, had higher ideals. They believed Paris conferred some special grace that favored the artist; that "in the city of boulevard bars and Baudelaire," as Alice Toklas put it, "writing was a contagious craft," to be contracted like a virus by simply breathing air thick with French tobacco, drinking unlimited red wine, and, above all, hanging out in cafés.

By the mid-1920s, every boat from New York brought

more writers hoping to eke out a living as journalists while they wrote a novel. Nineteen-year-old Kay Boyle, arriving in 1921 with her new husband, a French exchange student she'd met in her native Minnesota, embraced the conviction that "our life together was going to be a confirmation of our impatience with conventions and our commitment to something called Freedom, in which we believed so passionately." Fleeing the hostility of her bourgeois in-laws, she and her husband moved to a damp, cold cottage near Le Havre, where Boyle began to write but also contracted tuberculosis.

Not even Boyle, who had more reason to think so than most, believed herself part of a "lost generation." When Gertrude Stein popularized that term, she wasn't thinking of artists at all, but quoting a garage owner's criticism of a young mechanic who'd done a poor job repairing her car. Children brought up during the war, he lamented, lacked all ambition, and were thus *paumé*: an emotive word meaning "out of one's depth" or "godforsaken," but which Stein translated as simply "lost." Appropriate or not, the phrase, like "beat generation" and "summer of love," adhered as only a cliché can.

The first Americans to relocate in Paris were far from lost. They had money in their pockets and the leisure to spend it. Many wealthy nineteenth-century American families kept houses in France, and visited them annually. Brides had their wedding gowns made in Paris, purchased their silver and porcelain there, hired a French chef and maid. Men hunted in the forests around Paris, raced their horses, bought art, ate at its restaurants, and patronized its brothels.

Among twentieth-century expatriates, Gerald Murphy owned the Mark Cross chain of luxury outfitters. Harry Crosby was the nephew of financier J. Pierpont Morgan. Composer Cole Porter married a millionairess. Natalie Clifford Barney's family owned railroads, Gertrude Stein and her brothers had an interest in San Francisco mass transit, while Annie Winifred Ellerman and Nancy Cunard came from British shipping fortunes. In the large Spanish colony, Pablo Picasso was already becoming prosperous, and both Luis Buñuel and Salvador Dalí were sons of landed gentry.

Nor were Americans the most numerous foreigners in France. Uncounted Italians were imported to rebuild Paris in the wake of the Franco-Prussian War of 1870–71 and the modernizations dictated by Baron Haussmann. In 1917, a wave of 200,000 educated and aristocratic Russians fled the Bolsheviks to take refuge in France, their spiritual home.

Other newcomers owed their allegiance less to any one nation than to new styles of thought. Until 1917, Lenin,

Trotsky, and other architects of the Russian revolution lived and plotted in Montparnasse, traditionally a haven for anarchists and Communists. A different group embraced Tristan Tzara's Dada movement. Founded in Zurich during the war, it migrated to Paris with its founder, where it metamorphosed into Surrealism. The provocative theories of its founder, André Breton, attracted followers of wildly miscellaneous temperaments, and social and cultural backgrounds. "There is absolutely no reason," said Jean-Claude Carrière, screenwriter for Luis Buñuel, "why Benjamin Péret came from Toulouse to join the group, why Max Ernst comes from Germany, why and how Man Ray comes from the States and Buñuel from Spain, and they meet at last in Paris. But something was calling them together."

Those Anglophones who came to Paris hoping to make a living from journalism faced an uphill battle. Paris supported the *Paris Herald*, the *Paris Times*, and an edition of the *Chicago Tribune*, as well as society and fashion magazines like *Vogue*, but jobs on such publications were jealously guarded. The larger American and British publications already employed Paris correspondents. Sisley Huddleston represented the *Christian Science Monitor* and London *Times*, and Janet Flanner, as "Genêt," sent fortnightly reports to *The New Yorker*, though the most prolific commentator was Wambly Bald, a tireless gossip whom Henry Miller calls "Van Norden" in *Tropic of Cancer*.

One grabbed jobs where one could. Expatriates became translators, chauffeurs, language teachers, gigolos. Man Ray shot erotic photographs to order. Henry Miller wrote advertising for a Montparnasse brothel. Like the restaurants for which others translated menus and whose walls hungry painters decorated with art, the bordello paid in "trade." This suited Miller, for whom sex was at least as essential as bread.

Some arrangements were even less conventional. "I worked first for a film producer who also ran a racing stable," recalled Hungarian-born writer Emeric Pressburger, later the partner of British filmmaker Michael Powell. "Friends told me to learn the names of some horses he owned, and look in the paper to see when they were running. With some others to whom he also owed money, I'd go to the racetrack, and if the horse won we'd ask to be paid. And he would put his large hand—he was a large man—into his pocket, which was full of bank-notes, take out a handful, and say, 'Count that.'"

Harold Stearns, editor of *The New Republic* and *The Dial*, author of *Civilization in the United States*, and model for the alcoholic Harvey Stone in *The Sun Also Rises*, also spent much of his time at the racetrack, first as a gambler, then as tipster "Peter Pickem," with his own newspaper column. Prosperous friends gave him money to bet on their behalf. One of the strangest inscriptions in any copy of the James Joyce symposium *Our Exagmination Round His Factification for Incamination of Work in Progress* was penned by Harry Crosby to Stearns. "Here is the book I told you about," he wrote, adding, "Hope you didn't play our grubstake yesterday at Chantilly."

It stretches the *Casablanca* metaphor to equate Sylvia Beach with Humphrey Bogart. All the same, her little bookshop and lending library at 12 rue de l'Odéon did serve, like Rick's, as the exiles' post office, information bureau, and clubhouse. And since, when writers meet, they often break into print, Beach also became a publisher. It was a role for which she was ill suited by both temperament and fortune. Publishing in Paris, with few exceptions, was a hobby, and an expensive one. Harry Crosby's family money financed his Black Sun Press. Edward Titus's Black Manikin tapped the resources of his wife, beauty products manufacturer Helena Rubinstein. Nancy Cunard's Hours Press owed its existence to the family shipping line. Gay publisher Robert McAlmon agreed to marry Annie Winifred Ellerman, alias "Bryher," lesbian daughter of England's richest man of the time, Sir John Ellerman. His daughter now free to live openly in Paris with her companion, poet Hilda Doolittle, aka "H.D.," Ellerman bankrolled McAlmon's Contact Editions.

Lacking such patronage, Beach was forced to finance *Ulysses* by subscription. Robert McAlmon combed Montparnasse on her behalf, badgering people into signing order forms and, on the way home to his apartment lower down rue de l'Odéon, shoving what he called "a hasty bunch" under the door of Shakespeare and Company. The term became so associated with him that, at the suggestion of James Joyce, he called his first collection of short stories *A Hasty Bunch*.

A few publishers, among them Jack Kahane of the erotic Obelisk Press, strove for best-selling books, though as much to maximize their libertarian impact as to make money. Smaller presses chose the opposite path, publishing expensive limited editions aimed at collectors. Often working with antiquated presses, one sheet of handmade paper at a time, they seldom printed more than two hundred copies and sometimes as few as fifty. A single lapse of concentration could be disastrous. When the Three Mountains Press of journalist Bill Bird published Hemingway's *in our time*, an error in the choice of paper made half the first printing unsalable. Bird finally sold his hundred-year-old Mathieu press and its Caslon type to Nancy Cunard, who used them to create the books of her Hours Press.

Small presses survived on the avant-garde and scraps from established writers, who always had short or contentious texts that lent themselves to limited circulation. Black Sun published D. H. Lawrence's *The Escaped Cock*, a title that, for some reason, more conventional presses shunned. Other authors, accustomed to a 10 percent royalty, welcomed the more generous split on a limited edition, as much as 60/40 in their favor, even if it meant writing for a moneyed elite. Sylvia Beach embraced this method. Most copies of the first printing of *Ulysses* went to collectors who could afford the price—the equivalent, one English schoolteacher complained, of his monthly salary.

Not all authors displayed the greed of James Joyce, which left Beach bankrupt. A few, like Robert M. Coates, author of the Surrealist novel *The Eater of Darkness*, regarded their books as labors of love, from which it was inappropriate to profit. Others were dilettantes who just wanted their work in print, and would pay for the privilege. The urge to publish could afflict anyone. Though Waverley Root, literary editor of the Paris *Chicago Tribune*, disparaged the productions of such presses as Contact Editions, which he stigmatized as "dedicated to publishing the work of McAlmon himself and his closest friends," even he dabbled, financing a 1932 limited edition of Mark Twain's long-suppressed scatological *1601*, a parody of manners at the court of Queen Elizabeth I.

One solution to the small presses' problem of cash flow was the "little magazine." A literary quarterly, mixing short fiction, poetry, commentary, and illustration, could include as much material as a book but cost less to produce and, sold by subscription through the mail, bypassed bookshops, cutting out the middleman. Among such magazines, *transition*, edited by Eugene Jolas but backed and distributed by Sylvia Beach, was the undoubted star. Had it done no more than serialize Joyce's *Finnegans Wake* as *Work in Progress*, its importance would have been assured. Other periodicals included *Contact*, edited by Robert McAlmon and the poet William Carlos Williams, *Broom* of Harold Loeb, original of the character Robert Cohn in *The Sun Also Rises*, and *This Quarter*, launched by Ernest Walsh and later published by Edward Titus.

The reticent and scholarly Titus could not have differed more from the American poet who started *This Quarter* and edited the first two issues. "There was something very fine about Ernest Walsh," wrote Sylvia Beach. "He was alive and he was heroic." Since 1922, Walsh, who preferred to be called "Michael," had produced *This Quarter* with money from his older, wealthier wife, the painter Ethel Moorhead.

They lived in Grasse, above the Côte d'Azur, where Walsh went in hopes of curing his tuberculosis. D. H. Lawrence, seeking similar relief, had died there, but the promise of its clean and thin air continued to draw many, including Kay Boyle, who left her husband in Le Havre to move there.

Meeting Walsh, Boyle was immediately infatuated. When Moorhead, on dipping into her copy of Frank Harris's *My Life and Loves*, "looked at me severely in the eyes and asked if I could tell her what the word 'orgasm' meant," Boyle saw her opportunity. "Nothing mattered to me except Michael's beauty and his courage," she said, "and I wanted to pay homage to what he was for all my life." With Moorhead's grudging consent, she and Walsh became lovers, and had a child. The trio moved to Paris, where Walsh hoped to establish himself as a poet, but illness won and he died in 1926 with both Moorhead and Boyle at his bedside.

AT THE SIGN OF THE BLACK MANIKIN, EDWARD TITUS'S BOOKSHOP

4 RUE DELAMBRE
(NOW THE POISSONNERIE DU DÔME)

In 1924, Edward Titus left the management of his wife's company and opened At the Sign of the Black Manikin. According to his friend Morley Callaghan, he "had grown tired of the opulent display, the chauffeurs and all the business detail that took up his time." The sepulchral shop and his apartment above it, both filled with rare books and manuscripts, were less a commercial proposition than a refuge.

It embarrassed Titus to be rich in a community of the poor. In cafés, he would always pay only his own bill, not from stinginess but because, in Callaghan's words, "if he ever gave in and picked up the tab just because he was rich, he would lose all caste with the people whose respect he wanted."

Rather than see *This Quarter* die with its founder, Titus took over the magazine and published it until 1932. Despite superior paper and binding, and the literary competitions with cash prizes that he funded, the issues he and co-editor Ezra Pound filled with translations of Russian, Italian, and other foreign literature attracted little attention, in marked contrast to such competitors as *transition*, which seldom paid contributors and was so cheaply produced it fell apart in one's hands but was nevertheless regarded as essential reading.

Titus also published twenty-five books under the Black Manikin imprint. Obscure rural reminiscences alternated with sensational titles designed to attract notoriety. These included Lawrence's *Lady Chatterley's Lover*, the memoirs of model Kiki of Montparnasse, with an introduction by Hemingway, and Baudelaire's *Little Poems in Prose*, translated by satanist and self-styled "Great Beast" Aleister Crowley. All were tarred with the brush of solemn good taste. One detail was symptomatic. Where other presses often enclosed limited editions in protective slipcases covered in marbled or gilded paper, Black Manikin books came in sleeves of plain gray cardboard, economical but dull.

HIRED HELP

I don't think the rate of exchange is always given its
proper importance as an element in the charm of Paris.
To be able to live well on very little money is the best
basis for the appreciation of beauty anywhere, and
I think we admired the city all the more because we
could now eat and drink almost as much as we liked.
JOHN GLASSCO, *MEMOIRS OF MONTPARNASSE*

ANYONE VISITING MONTPARNASSE AFTER 1900 WOULD
have been struck by the cosmopolitan stock of J. Hazard,
the quarter's largest grocery store. Occupying half a block
on Boulevard du Montparnasse, it announced prominently
over the door "English Spoken," while its goods reflected
the district's racial mix. "Americans find here their grapefruit, as little like a lemon as a watermelon resembles a
cantaloupe," said Apollinaire. "Russians find those Apples of

Paradise [i.e., pomegranates] that resemble [giant] bigarreau cherries, and the Hungarians their meats and sausages spiced with paprika." Not that many expatriates actually shopped at Hazard, or anywhere else. For that, they employed a maid of all work known as a *femme de ménage*. Servants of any kind scarcely rate a mention in memoirs of Paris. Even Gertrude Stein and Alice Toklas imply that dinner parties and Saturday evening soirées at rue de Fleurus took place with no outside help. Yet waiters, maids, cooks, nannies, drivers, secretaries, concierges, and housekeepers were as essential to life in France as Chinese laborers to the building of America's railroads.

Gertrude and Alice employed a succession of *femmes de ménage* and cooks, few of them satisfactory. Some absented themselves for months to spend time with lovers, while others, on being introduced to the kitchen, failed Alice's test of a cook, the ability to produce a good omelette. Another, after Gertrude's death, threatened Alice with blackmail over her paying to spring their collaborator friend Bernard Fay from prison and spirit him to Switzerland.

The cheap franc made home help accessible to the poorest expatriate. Lillian Maddock, hired at the end of 1922 by Scott and Zelda Fitzgerald as nanny for their daughter Scotty, was paid $26 a month, at a time when the going rate in New York was closer to $80. A *femme de ménage* earned far less, but there was no shortage of applicants. The war, followed by the 1919 influenza epidemic, wiped out millions of young men, leaving France with a disproportionate number of widows and single women with little hope of marrying. Country-born, most willingly traded rural tedium for the vitality of Paris and a job in service, however poorly paid.

Even Ernest and Hadley Hemingway, when they scraped along on $1,000 a year, could afford a housekeeper. Her name was Marie Rohrbach and she came from Brittany. When they lived in two rooms on rue du Cardinal-Lemoine, she arrived each morning to make breakfast, stayed to clean house, washed, ironed, and mended clothes, shopped, then returned to prepare an evening meal. After the birth of John, aka Bumby, she became his nursemaid, and remained with Hadley after the divorce.

Life for her was less demanding than for many domestics, since the Hemingways were often out of town. Even so, her work, without the benefit of laborsaving appliances, was punishing. Everything they ate or used had to be carried up four flights of stairs. She ironed with heavy flatirons heated on the stove, scrubbed floors on her hands and knees

Ernest Hemingway with son John, aka Bumby.

with a stiff brush, then polished them by shuffling through the rooms with rags tied to her feet. In old age, both her legs would be amputated, partly the result, Hadley believed, of such grinding labor.

Even with the pittance they paid her, Hemingway could grumble in a letter at the end of 1925 that "Bumby has an expensive nurse." He did eventually concede Marie a paragraph in "The Education of Mr. Bumby," a chapter cut from what became *A Moveable Feast*.

> *Bumby would pass those months with the* femme de ménage *who he called Touton [actually "Tonton"] either at 10 bis Avenue des Gobelins where they had a flat or at [the Breton village of] Mûr-de-Bretagne where they went for monsieur Rohrbach's summer vacations. Monsieur Rohrbach had been a* maréchal des logis—chef *or sergeant major in the professional French military establishment and on his retirement had a minor functionary post on which they had lived with his and Marie's wages and looked forward to his retirement to Mûr-de-Bretagne. Touton had a great part in the formative years of Bumby's life.*

After the divorce, Hemingway's new wife, Pauline, met Marie in the Luxembourg Gardens with Bumby, and tried to hire her. "Marie is cockeyed to come to work for us," she wrote to Ernest, but Hadley angrily quashed the idea. For a woman with a young child, a servant was indispensable. "I was so pleased about getting a good cook," Pauline admitted, "that I didn't consider the ramifications."

HEMINGWAY'S CONCIERGE

69 RUE FROIDEVAUX
(NOW AN APARTMENT BUILDING)

One other class of servant influenced life in Paris. Fount of local knowledge, repository of social history, a tireless gossip who combined a private detective's inquisitiveness with a criminal's cunning, the concierge was as much an institution as the café. Fewer in number today, they still observe who comes and goes in their building, the twitch of a curtain on the window of their loge a reminder that little happens without their knowledge and tacit consent. A nineteenth-century description captured their often malign influence.

The concierge's loge was the hub of a spider's net, its threads reached not only into every apartment in the building but extending out in the street. The tenants were well-advised to remain on her good side. Failing that, their mail could go astray, and their reputation be tarnished by malicious gossip through the neighborhood. Her eagle-eye noticed all

*the comings and goings, especially past ten
o'clock in the evening, when the main door was
locked and late comers must ring the bell.*

Originally a man's job, the role of concierge
passed in the twentieth century to women who were
prepared to become virtual prisoners of a building
in return for a tiny apartment in it. Typically middle-
aged, often foreign, and generally living alone except for a cat or bird, they belied the supposedly
casual French attitude to promiscuity by posing as
stern moralists. When Scots painter Gwen John and
two friends moved into a studio on rue Froidevaux
at the turn of the century, the concierge warned
them about visitors. "Other ladies, yes. But men.
Never!" Concierges seldom had either the time or
inclination for sex, a fact that puts a question mark
next to an incident described in Hemingway's posthumous novel *True at First Light.*

Assembled by his heirs, *True at First Light* describes Hemingway's disastrous East African safari
of 1954–55, interrupted by two plane crashes that
he and his fourth wife, Mary, barely survived. Flash-
backs illuminate incidents in Ernest's life in Paris.
One episode, dating from his split with Hadley in

the spring of 1926, describes the seven months he spent in a studio apartment at 69 rue Froidevaux.

The Hemingways had been holidaying with the Murphys in Pamplona when Hadley, furious at Ernest's flagrant affair with Pauline Pfeiffer, demanded a divorce, and returned to Paris alone. Ernest wrote, "I went to Gerald Murphy's sixth-floor studio at 69 rue Froidevaux, which he had offered to me. Also, knowing I was broke, he slipped 400 bucks into my checking account at the Morgan Guaranty, which I used to repay some debts."

Rue Froidevaux borders the Cimetière du Montparnasse, its northern side the graveyard wall: not a location to attract everyone, though both Alberto Giacometti and Robert Capa lived there at various times. Hemingway says he took no interest in his view, mainly a vista of roofs. His first weeks were spent correcting the proofs of *The Sun Also Rises*, and, he claimed, not answering the door to anyone. But *True at First Light* tells a different story.

> At that time my concierge was my girl. I had never known a young concierge before and it was an inspiring experience. Her greatest asset

was that she could never go out, not only in society, but at all.

I was not in love with my concierge but I was very lonely at night at that time and the first time she came up the stairs and through the door, which had a key in it, and then up the ladder that led to the sort of loft where the bed was beside the window that gave such a lovely view over the Cemetery Montparnasse and took off her felt-soled shoes and lay on the bed and asked me if I loved her.

I answered, loyally, "Naturally."

"I knew it," she said. "I've known it too long."

She undressed quickly and I looked out at the moonlight on the cemetery.... She was clean and fragile out of sturdy but insufficient nourishment and we paid honor to the view which neither saw. I had it in my mind however and then she said that the last tenant had entered.

Like most anecdotes about Hemingway's later love life, this one can't be authenticated. (One skeptic, employing a metaphor appropriate to an author enamored of the corrida, remarked, "As a writer, Hemingway works very close to the bull.")

All the same, its details ring true. Studios, generally converted from former maids' rooms, were often "loft-like." Felt-soled slippers were standard for domestics, while a concierge could never go out or leave her post by the front door until the last tenant had entered.

After Pauline leased an apartment on rue Ferou, near the Luxembourg Gardens, Ernest left her to clean out the studio while he went driving with a friend through Italy. She remembered it only as full of books and papers. If there was any trace of a complaisant young concierge, she isn't mentioned.

A concierge. (Marcel Poncin)

THE OTHER BOHEMIANS

The day is coming when a single carrot,
freshly observed, will set off a revolution.
PAUL CÉZANNE

Once the artists of Montmartre began to make money, most abandoned its squalid and often violent streets. Some moved to the bourgeois district below Boulevard de Clichy known as the New Athens. Others gravitated to Montparnasse, but, as early as 1914, Guillaume Apollinaire intuited from the kind of people who relocated there that it would always be more playground than workshop. Most, he wrote, came from "the Montmartre of artists, singers, windmills, cabarets—which also means, of course, that all the hashish-eaters, opium smokers and the inevitable sniffers of ether, plus anyone else who's been expelled from a Montmartre being destroyed by landlords and architects, have moved, along with people of the same kind, wherever they come from."

His forecast, if tactless, was accurate. Although local painters, among them Jules Pascin, Tsuguharu Foujita, Francis Picabia, Chaim Soutine, and Kees van Dongen would form what became known as the School of Paris, serious artists in Montparnasse were outnumbered by students and hobby painters, writers and musicians, frequently foreign, and a floating population of loafers and drifters. Many congregated around the independent art academies that sprouted on a narrow and obscure street running downhill from Boulevard du Montparnasse to rue Notre-Dame-des-Champs. As a reminder of the *bal jardin* that once stood there, it was called rue de la Grande-Chaumière.

For centuries, the serious study of art, aside from the private tuition of various artists and a few schools such as Académie Julian, took place primarily at the École des Beaux-Arts. Founded in 1648 by Cardinal-Duke Jules Raymond Mazarin, a famous connoisseur and collector, its premises on rue Bonaparte, within sight of the Louvre, were both geographically and culturally far from Montparnasse.

The Beaux-Arts taught that painting, sculpture, and architecture had barely advanced in a millennium. Students spent their first year sketching plaster casts of classic

Some Montparnos, including Foujita, 1929. (Sem)

sculpture or memorizing elements of Greco-Roman design. Even when they moved on to life classes, so-called *modèles de profession* copied their poses from the same antique statues and reliefs, and became indignant if asked to behave more naturally.

Candidates for the Beaux-Arts had first to demonstrate superior talent. Once admitted and having paid their hefty tuition, they were required to buy all their materials, including an easel of approved style and two rush-bottom stools. The administration also levied a weekly charge, known as *le masse,* to cover models' fees, lighting, cleaning, soap, towels, and turpentine. Within the school, a ruthless

pecking order prevailed. In life classes, seniors monopolized
the front seats. Freshmen—the Beaux-Arts didn't admit
women—were also expected to run errands for the seniors,
and clean their studios. In the sculpture and architecture
schools, they swept floors, acted as porters, and broke down
clay models at the end of class, remixing the material for use
the following day, an exhausting and degrading task.

Once a week, a master visited each class to assess its
work. A few students became protégés, privileged to assist
their tutors with personal projects in return for private
tuition. Making all this bearable was the professionally
precious diploma, and the possibility, in their final year, of
winning the Prix de Rome and spending a year in travel, all
expenses paid.

Students of the Beaux-Arts advertised their elite status, even to the way they dressed. A visitor described "the
genuine type of French student, with his long hair, his
whiskers, his Latin Quarter 'plug' hat, his cape, blouse,
wide corduroy trousers, sash, expensive necktie, and
immense cane. The École preserves this type more
effectually than the other schools, such as Julian's and
Colarossi's, where most of the students are foreigners in
conventional dress."

By 1900, however, a third of the Beaux-Arts students

New student at the École des Beaux-Arts, with equipment. (Édouard Cucuel)

were also foreigners, many of them American, and increasingly impatient with its methods. They looked toward Montparnasse, to the Académie de la Grande-Chaumière, the Académie Carmen, and in particular the Académie Colarossi, started in 1870 by sculptor Filippo Colarossi.

Paul Gauguin, sculptor Camille Claudel, and couturier Paul Poiret were all associated with Colarossi's. Foreign students included German-American Lyonel Feininger and German George Grosz. Some teachers were expatriates themselves. Alphonse Mucha, Czech master of the swirling art nouveau style, anathema to the Beaux-Arts, taught a popular course at Colarossi's, which in 1911 appointed its first female teacher, and an expatriate as well, New Zealand artist Frances Hodgkins.

In 1898, James McNeill Whistler helped his favorite model, Carmen Rossi, start her own Montparnasse school, the Académie Carmen. He taught there until 1901, a magnet for American students, particularly young women, whom Rossi charged double, a common practice among art schools, which argued that most females were just dilettantes and cluttered up the system. Rossi, who knew the women, predominantly American and well-off, would happily pay for the Whistler glamour, restored equality under pressure from Whistler, but students were soon challenging her other rules, such as no smoking, no singing in the halls, no talking in class, not to mention her imposition of the hated *masse*.

One Beaux-Arts professor dismissed the new schools as "a ramshackle set of studios where artists and students could pay to use the models and receive a little tutoring if they wished," but instructors found their informality exhilarating. "My class is a meeting point for international youth who are investigating the new world of forms," wrote Russian sculptor Ossip Zadkine, who taught at Grande-Chaumière. "At each master class I hold on Fridays between

Whistler with students at Académie Carmen. (Cyrus Cuneo)

10 am and 12 pm, there is a horde of foreign nationals who come to hear what I have to say. These young people are very heart-warming, but I leave as tired as if I'd just gone down with a cold."

Colarossi's and Grande-Chaumière levied fees only for their morning sculpture courses, taught by such established figures as Zadkine and Antoine Bourdelle. Those attending afternoon and evening sketching classes paid by the session: as little as fifty centimes; less than a horse bus ride, and cheaper still if they bought tickets by the booklet. Men and women were equally welcome, nor was there an entry requirement. A Sunday painter from the suburbs could find himself drawing the same model as Amedeo Modigliani, a regular at Colarossi's when he was not in the Rotonde, doing portraits for a franc a time and drinking away the money. It was at Colarossi's that he met Jeanne Hébuterne, the mistress and model who, distraught at his death in 1920, would kill herself and their unborn child.

Other innovations at the new schools included evening sessions under electric light, though the atmosphere at these, attended by people who often came directly from work and seldom changed their clothes, was oppressive. "All the rooms were packed," protested Russian painter Marevna Vorobiev. "In the one where we were drawing from the nude, the air was stifling because of an overheated

Life class at Académie Colarossi.

stove. We were positively melting in an inferno perme-
ated by the strong smell of perspiring bodies mixed with
scent, fresh paint, damp waterproofs and dirty feet; all
this was intensified by the thick smoke from cigarettes and
the strong tobacco of pipe smokers." Artists at some classes
complained there was so much smoke that, from the back
rows, they could barely see the model.

Female students faced other difficulties. Scots artist
Kathleen Bruce described her first day at Colarossi's in
1901. "At the end of the studio passed, one by one, a string
of nude male models. Each jumped for a moment on to the
model throne, took a pose and jumped down. The model

for the day was being chosen. Before reason could control instinct, I turned and fled, shut myself in the lavatory, and was sick." The men probably weren't completely naked, male models usually wearing a posing pouch, but the effect on conservative young women was the same. Bruce survived and became a successful artist. Others fled, adopting the impressionists' preference for painting *en plein air*.

Art supply stores and rooming houses sprang up along rue de la Grande-Chaumière, as well as a number of *crèmeries*: sellers of dairy products who diversified into serving cheap food. The Crèmerie Leduc on Boulevard Raspail was popular, but the tiny Crèmerie Caron, opposite the Académie Colarossi, was even cheaper, and a favorite with Modigliani, Mucha, and Gauguin. Its plump proprietor, Charlotte Caron, widow of an Alsatian soldier killed during the Franco-Prussian War, sometimes accepted paintings in payment. They decorated the restaurant and the rooms above, which she rented to, among others, Gauguin and Mucha. In return for meals, Mucha and the Polish artist Władysław Ślewiński decorated the metal panels of her façade, Mucha's painting advertising *"Purée artistique"* (Artistic Mashed Potatoes).

Art schools proliferated in Montparnasse, some long-lived, others surviving only a season. André Lhote taught at 26 rue du Départ. The Académie du Montparnasse was at 10 rue de l'Arrivée, the Académie du Caméleo at 241 Boulevard Raspail, Académie Szabo at 22 rue Delambre, and Académie Ranson, founded in 1908 by the painter Paul Ranson, at 7 rue Joseph-Bara.

The Académie Carmen closed in 1901 when Whistler became too ill to continue teaching. Others survived into the 1930s. In 1935, Nora, daughter of Australian artist Hans Heysen, wrote of rue de la Grande-Chaumière that "every shop almost in this little street sells artists' materials, and opposite is the atelier where Bourdelle the sculptor and Lucien Simon teach. The art shops down the street are marvellous, crammed from door to ceiling with canvases and sketchbooks, and great jars of brushes and so forth."

Despite their importance in the history of art, documentation of these schools is skimpy. The Beaux-Arts maintained meticulous archives but the Montparnos professed a bohemian indifference to keeping records. The wife of Filippo Colarossi did document their school, even preserving work by the most gifted students. However, she lost patience with her husband's philandering and, just before it finally closed, in a classic Montparnasse gesture, burned everything.

THE MODEL MARKET

CORNER OF BOULEVARD DU MONTPARNASSE
AND RUE DE LA GRANDE-CHAUMIÈRE

In 1880, 671 women between the ages of sixteen and twenty were registered as artists' models in Montmartre alone. Twenty years later, most had moved to Montparnasse, where a "model market" convened each Monday at the corner of Boulevard du Montparnasse and rue de la Grande-Chaumière. Jean Émile-Bayard described "Italian *modelos*, matrons from Naples and elsewhere, Levantines and blacks, *Carmencitas* and ex-seamstresses, a seething carnival with its pretty girls and proud adolescents, its decrepit peasants and old men with white beards nursing their grandchildren, all ready to inspire painters and artists."

Modeling was hard work, requiring a knowledge of classic poses and the ability to hold them for hours at a time. It was, however, well paid: five francs for three hours, at a time when a laborer was lucky to earn that in a week. Most artists could only afford a model if a number shared the cost. Many women improved their chances by offering a sexual bonus, redeemable in the rooming houses along rue Huyghens, near the cemetery, where concierges turned a blind eye for a few sous.

In this promiscuous culture, both tuberculosis and sexually transmitted diseases were rampant. Modigliani was one of many artists who died of the former, while, until Ehrlich's discovery of a cure in 1910, an estimated 10 percent of Montparnos suffered from syphilis. A model known as Rosa la Rouge (Rosa the Red) infected many, including Henri de Toulouse-Lautrec, who died aged thirty-seven. Other sufferers included Édouard Manet, Guy de Maupassant, and Charles Baudelaire. Composer Frederick Delius and Vladimir Lenin both contracted the disease during their years in Montparnasse, as did Gauguin's Polish protégé Stanisław Wyspiański, and Gauguin himself, who would die of it in 1903.

In 1914, police shut down the model market after shopkeepers and restaurateurs complained it was impeding business by blocking sidewalks. Perhaps it was, but their reasons were more self-serving. While bohemia was not yet respectable, Montparnasse sensed its commercial value. Instead of giving it away on the street, it could be sold for hard cash in bars, hotels, and cafés.

Models outside Académie de la Grande-Chaumière. (Georges Leroux)

SVENGALI

Montparnasse, in the opinion of people
living nearby, is a quarter of crazies.
GUILLAUME APOLLINAIRE, 1914

Among the most potent advertisements for bohemian Paris was George du Maurier's 1894 novel *Trilby*. Its heroine, the innocent young Irish model Trilby O'Ferrall, is transformed by hypnosis into a great singer. The "well-featured but sinister man of Jewish aspect" who engineers this metamorphosis calls himself Svengali. Far from glamorizing him, du Maurier emphasized his repulsiveness.

> *He was very shabby and dirty, and wore a red*
> *béret and a large velveteen cloak, with a big metal*
> *clasp at the collar. His thick, heavy, languid,*
> *lustreless black hair fell down behind his ears on to*

his shoulders, in that musician-like way that is so
offensive to the normal Englishman. He had bold,
brilliant black eyes, with long, heavy lids, a thin,
sallow face, and a beard of burnt-up black which
grew almost from his under eyelids; and over it his
mustache, a shade lighter, fell in two long spiral
twists.

Trilby romanticized Montparnasse to a generation of readers, predominantly female, just as *Dracula* promoted the erotic lure of vampirism. To social historian Luc Santé, du Maurier's book "affected the habits of American youth, particularly young women, who derived from it the courage to call themselves artists and 'bachelor girls,' to smoke cigarettes and drink Chianti." Under its influence, they looked to Paris to satisfy that perverse urge to embrace degradation and depravity the French call *la nostalgie de la boue*: a yearning for the mud. Romantic novelists like Marie Corelli, Ouida, and E. M. Hull traded on these urges. In the film of Hull's *The Sheik*, Rudolph Valentino as glamorous Arab Ahmed ben Hassan—Paris-educated, naturally—carries off an English aristocrat to his desert camp. When she quavers, "Why have you brought me here?" and he responds, *"Mon dieu!* Are you not woman enough to know?" audiences, both male and female, shivered—not in fear, but anticipation.

Montparnasse had no shortage of Svengali look-alikes. One was Paul Gauguin, on whom du Maurier may have modeled the character. Peruvian blood gave him the bold nose and high cheekbones of an Aztec idol. With his Mephistophelian beard and mustache, long oily black hair and huge liquid eyes, he epitomized unquenchable creativity, an appetite for life.

Herbert Beerbohm Tree as Svengali.

Mucha met him for the first time at Crèmerie Caron. "Madame Charlotte introduced him as a sailor who was also a painter: a powerfully built Breton, dressed in something that looked like a national costume. On his head he wore an astrakhan cap and across his shoulders a wide cloak with ornamental clasps." Discovering a mutual enthusiasm for dressing up, they spent hours in Mucha's studio above the *crèmerie*, photographing each other in exotic outfits against the background of the Aladdin's cave into which Mucha had transformed it. Between sessions, Gauguin played selections from Wagner on the harmonium.

Cruising the music halls and bars of rue de la Gaîté, drinking at the Aux Îles Marquises and buying pigments at the store next door, they were often joined by Guillaume Apollinaire, who had supported the Cubists and was attempting to do the same for Henri Rousseau, so poor he was reduced to playing the violin in the street. He died in 1910, still unknown, and unable to afford the medical care that would have saved his life. Buried in a pauper's grave, his body was exhumed in 1913 after a posthumous exhibition at the Salon des Indépendants made his reputation. For the new grave, sculptor Constantin Brâncuşi carved a portrait plaque and Apollinaire composed an epitaph for "Le Douanier":

Let our luggage pass duty-free through the gates of
    heaven.
We will bring you brushes, paints, and canvas
That you may spend your sacred leisure in the light
    and truth of painting.

The culture of Montparnasse was the first in which Gauguin felt at home. He'd traveled the world as a seaman, living briefly in Peru, Panama, and Martinique, but left each of them sick and destitute. Needing to support his Danish wife and four children, he joined a Paris investment bank, but failed also as a broker. When his Danish relatives made it clear he was no longer welcome in Copenhagen, he returned gratefully to Paris and the world of art.

Late in 1891, Gauguin sailed for Polynesia. Two years later, loaded with new work but penniless, he returned to a city deserted for the summer vacation. Fortunately, Mucha was still in town, and offered him space in his studio to prepare the forty-six paintings and eleven sculptures shown at Paul Durand-Ruel's gallery in November 1893.

At a time when the French state encouraged "history paintings" that celebrated national achievement, these mystical visions of peasant Brittany, with their stylized crucifixions and angels, and above all his sensual celebration of the South Seas and its women, could not have been less fashionable. One reviewer wrote, "To amuse the children, send them to the Gauguin show. They'll get a laugh out of the brightly colored images of women with four hands lying on billiard-table cloth, the whole thing garnished with rude words."

Even his impressionist friends disapproved. "He's not a seer, he's a schemer," said Camille Pissarro, suspecting his onetime protégé of pandering to the French admiration of tribal people, whom they saw as the unspoiled "natural men" celebrated by Jean-Jacques Rousseau. But Gauguin, unapologetic, reveled in trampling barriers. He told a friend:

> *I have done a self-portrait for Vincent [van Gogh], who asked me for it. I believe it is one of my best things: so abstract it's (believe me!) absolutely incomprehensible. It looks at first like the head of a bandit, a Jean Valjean [the hounded hero of* Les Misérables*], but it also personifies a disreputable impressionist painter, burdened forever with the ball and chain of existence. The drawing is altogether peculiar, being completely abstract. The eyes, the mouth, the nose are like the pattern in a Persian carpet, thus personifying also the symbolical side.*

The colour is a colour remote from nature; imagine something like the glaze on a pot twisted by the furnace! All the reds and violets streaked like flames, as in a furnace burning fiercely, the seat of the painter's mental struggles. The whole on a chrome yellow background sprinkled with childish nosegays, like the wallpaper in the bedroom of a pure young girl—or of an impressionist not yet sullied by the filthy kiss of the Beaux-Arts.

A month after the exhibition, Gauguin received the windfall of a FF13,000 inheritance. Even after sharing with his wife, there remained enough to move out of Madam Charlotte's and rent two rooms on the top floor of 6 rue Vercingétorix. Deciding that, if he could not go to the South Seas, he would bring the South Seas to Paris, he painted its walls the vivid chrome yellow to which he'd become sensitized in the brief time spent with van Gogh in Arles, and filled the apartment with tribal art. To Polynesian carvings, he added his own ceramics, and sculptures in both wood and stone. He even carved and colored his wooden clogs. Paintings covered the windows, over one of which he lettered in pidgin Tahitian *"Ici faruru"*: Here we make love. On Thursday evenings, friends gathered in his apartment or that of Mucha to play music, sing, smoke,

Paul Gauguin's self-portrait, painted for Vincent van Gogh.

dress up, and photograph one another. Edvard Munch, August Strindberg, and Delius were sometimes joined by Aristide Maillol and Maurice Ravel.

It took Gauguin two years to raise enough money to return to Polynesia. In June 1895, he made his last voyage, first to Tahiti, then to the Marquesas, where he died in 1903. Above the door to his house there, he carved *"Maison du Jouir"* (House of Orgasm), while two panels flanking it articulated his philosophy of life: *"Soyez mystérieuses"* (Be mysterious) and *"Soyez amoureuses et vous serez heureuses"* (Be amorous and you will be happy).

ANNAH LA JAVANAÏSE
APARTMENT OF PAUL GAUGUIN

6 RUE VERCINGÉTORIX

In 1893, staff at the Gare de Lyon were puzzled by the appearance of a petite dark-skinned teenager, speaking no known language and accompanied only by a tiny red monkey. A label around her neck gave the address of opera singer Nina Pack and the cryptic note *"Envoi de Java"* (Sent from Java).

Once she was delivered, Pack recalled that, during a tour of the Far East, she had mentioned wanting an Asian maid. Apparently a friend had obliged. Pack called the girl Anna or Annah, but, when she proved a flop as a maid, turned her out into the street. Art dealer Ambroise Vollard, knowing Gauguin's exotic tastes, suggested she might make a good model. "Send her to me," the painter said. "I'll try her out." He did so with the painting known as *Annah la Javanaïse* (though by then he'd discovered she actually came from Sri Lanka).

Annah was about thirteen in 1893 when she posed for this famous canvas. Inspired by *Olympia*, Manet's controversial depiction of a chill, pale prostitute reclining nude on a couch, it showed Annah lounging naked in an outsized Chinese chair, with her monkey, named Taoa, by her feet. Gauguin had hoped that Judith, thirteen-year-old daughter of his neighbor, Norwegian composer William Molard, would pose for the picture. Precociously sexual, she would gladly have done so, and more, had her mother, the sculptor Ida Ericsson, not forbidden it. Substituting Annah, Gauguin gave her the same challenging stare as Manet's whore, but added a testy Tahitian subtitle to the painting: *Aita Parari te Tamari Vahine Judith*: The Child Judith Is Not Yet Breached [i.e., considered to be a woman].

Gauguin took Annah with him to Brittany but when the superstitious locals decided she was a witch and pelted her with stones, sent her back to Paris with the key to the apartment. He returned to find her gone, having sold his furniture, though not his paintings and carvings, which dealers, fortunately, thought worthless.

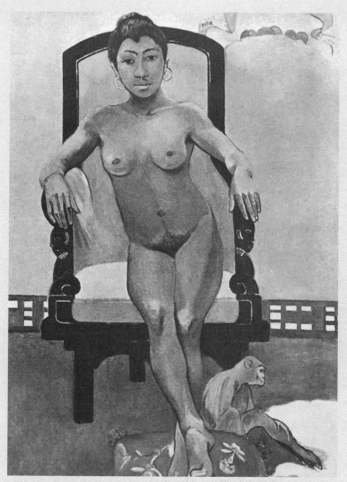

Annah la Javanaïse. *(Paul Gauguin)*

✹ · 7 · ✹

ABSINTHE AND ALCHEMY

CLOSERIE DES LILAS

Why don't you take some absinthe? Are you afraid of it? Look at the bottle! It's marked with the Geneva [Red] cross! It heals those who have been wounded on the battlefield, friends and foes alike; it dulls all pain, blunts the keen edge of thought, blots out memories, stifles all the nobler emotions which beguile humanity into folly, and finally extinguishes the light of reason.
AUGUST STRINDBERG, *INFERNO*

MODERN VISITORS PASSING THROUGH THE HEDGE SUR-rounding the Closerie des Lilas seldom know anything of the establishment except Hemingway's praise of it as "one of the best cafés in Paris. It was warm inside in the winter and in the spring and fall it was fine outside with the table

under the shade of the trees on the side where the statue of
Marshal Ney was, and the square, regular tables under the
big awnings along the boulevard."

Over the half century following the closing of La
Californie and the other eating houses along the customs
wall, Montparnasse coffee had not improved beyond the
"hot water, black in color, for a sou a cup" served in the
1850s. Among those who gathered here to drink it and
chat, it was fashionable to "correct" the bitter brew with
a shot of cognac.

The serious drink of the Closerie was absinthe, known,
because of its herby opalescence, as *la fée verte*: the green
fairy. Distilled from wormwood, fennel, licorice, and anise,
bolstered with as much as 74 percent alcohol, it was made
illegal in 1915 because of its debilitating and sometimes fatal
effects. Poets Charles Baudelaire and Paul Verlaine drank
it at the Closerie, Verlaine staggering home "just alive,"
recalled Alphonse Mucha, "swaying through the streets
in a flowing greatcoat, a pathetic wreck, living on the thin
ice of his reputation, honored and suffered by his shocked
admirers." Verlaine would die in a rooming house at 39
rue Descartes—the same building, by coincidence, where
Hemingway rented a garret workroom in 1922.

Another user, Swedish playwright August Strindberg,
confided to his diary for May 17, 1904, "Absinthe at six

Absinthe Drinkers. *(Edgar Degas)*

o'clock on the terrace of Brasserie des Lilas behind Marshal Ney has become my only vice, my last joy. Then, when the daily works are finished, body and soul weary, I will recover with the green drink, a cigarette, and *Le Temps* and *Journal des Débats*. How sweet life still is anyway, when a mild intoxication pulls its hazy veil over life's misery."

Strindberg was among a number of artistic Scandinavians who made Paris their home at the turn of the century. Aside from Gauguin's neighbors, William Molard and Ida Ericsson, Edvard Munch, of the famous *Scream*, studied there, absorbing the influence of Toulouse-Lautrec, van Gogh, and particularly Gauguin. Fellow Norwegian Per Krohg studied with Matisse in 1909 and 1910, and stayed on, becoming a familiar face around the quarter. British composer Frederick Delius, a friend and admirer of the Norwegian Edvard Grieg, joined their circle in 1888, becoming a friend of Munch, Gauguin, and, through Gauguin, Strindberg.

Miss Julie, Strindberg's 1888 play about the war of nerves between a willful middle-class woman and an intellectual servant, shook the European literary establishment. An admirer of naturalistic novelist and playwright Émile Zola, he was drawn to Paris by his presence, and an interest in alchemy. As Paris was a hub for this pseudoscience and the headquarters of such mystical sects as the Rosicrucians,

Strindberg determined to become "the Zola of the occult." Prowling the back streets of the city, he found its grave-yards particularly rich in "the emanations of the dead," so potent in the Cimetière du Montparnasse that he claimed to have transmuted its soil into gold. "He showed me pebbles entirely coated with the precious metal," said Delius, "and asked me to have one of these samples analyzed by an eminent chemist of my acquaintance. My friend examined it and found it to be covered with pure gold. He was hugely interested." But when Delius demanded more details, Strindberg said hurriedly it was too early to reveal his methods.

Increasingly addicted to absinthe, Strindberg became prey to hallucinations. Shortly after Verlaine died of its effects, Strindberg showed Delius a photograph of the poet on his deathbed and asked what he saw.

"Such as?"

"Well, the huge animal lying on his stomach," Strindberg said, puzzled at the other's obtuseness, "and the imp crouched on the floor!"

Reality and fantasy blurred. "Waiting for company for dinner," he wrote, "I sat on the sidewalk on the Boulevard Saint-Germain opposite the Cluny [Abbey Museum] and ordered an absinthe. Soon three figures arrived, I do not know from where, and stood before me. Two men with torn garments, sprayed with dirt as if they had just been pulled from the sewers, and beside them a woman, bare-headed, with tousled hair, traces of beauty, drunken, dirty. All stared at me with scornful looks, insolent, cynical, as if they knew me and waited to be invited to my table. Then it hit me: they're not real people!'"

He finally wore out his welcome with the Montparnos when he abused the hospitality of Charlotte Caron. Sneaking into the *crèmerie* at night, he used her cooking pots for an experiment in alchemy. She had to close down while everything was scoured of poisonous residues. Her clients rebelled. Scientific experiment was one thing but lunch took precedence. Persona non grata, Strindberg was seen less around Grande-Chaumière, and in time returned to Sweden.

Roller Skating at Bal Bullier, *1913. (Lucy Odero)*

STATUE OF MARSHAL MICHEL NEY, PLACE DE L'OBSERVATOIRE

CORNER OF BOULEVARD SAINT-MICHEL AND BOULEVARD DU MONTPARNASSE

Neither the Closerie des Lilas nor the same proprietor's Bal Bullier would have existed without the spectral patronage of Michel Ney. Napoleon's most able marshal, Ney rejoined the regular army after the emperor's exile to Elba in 1814, only to switch his allegiance back when Bonaparte escaped and returned to France for the "hundred days" that ended at Waterloo.

Following Napoleon's final exile to Saint Helena, Ney was tried for treason by the army he'd deserted, and shot in December 1815 as a warning to other officers who might be tempted to pick up where Napoleon left off. His execution, staged just opposite where the Closerie des Lilas now stands, deeply divided France. An officer to the last, Ney took command of the firing squad, and personally gave the order to shoot. In 1853, a penitent government commissioned a statue by François Rude that showed Ney, saber raised, leading his troops into battle, and added a plinth enumerating the achievements of a man Napoleon called "the bravest of the brave." Hemingway admired the monument. "He looked very fine, Marshal Ney in his top-boots, gesturing with his sword among the green new horse-chestnut leaves."

In 1868, Jean-Léon Gérôme exhibited his painting *L'exécution du maréchal Ney* at the annual Salon. It shows a firing squad marching away in the rain, leaving Ney's corpse, in civilian clothes, face-down in the mud, next to the wall where he was shot. The words *"Vive l'Empereur"* have been gouged into the plaster of the wall, then scratched out, to be replaced simply by the word *"Vive"*—Live.

The association with Ney made this intersection the ideal location for a coach stop on the road to Fontainebleau. Its first proprietor, François Bullier, planted a perfumed lilac hedge to shelter clients from the dust of the road and disguise the smell of horses. No sentimentalist, he also bought the wall against which Ney was shot, and built a dance hall, the Bal Bullier, behind it. Such stars of the Moulin Rouge as La Goulue, Grille d'Égout (Sewer Grating), and Valentin le Désossé (Boneless Valentin) danced there, but when the attraction of the cancan palled,

Bullier introduced the newest craze, roller skating. (A café opposite the Closerie calls itself the Bullier, but the original, as well as the wall against which Ney died, were demolished to build the monolithic Centre Sportif Universitaire Jean Sarrailh.)

The Execution of Marshal Ney. *(Jean-Léon Gérôme)*

8

A ROOM WITH A VIEW

A Clean, Well-Lighted Place
TITLE OF A SHORT STORY BY
ERNEST HEMINGWAY

Mainly known for painting battlefields and field hospitals during World War I, British artist C. R. W. Nevinson deserves a footnote in the history of the quarter for a single canvas, his 1926 *A Studio in Montparnasse*. Few images capture so seductively the dream of an artist's life. At a tall window overlooking the roofs of Montparnasse, a beautiful girl stands, naked, stroking a black cat. A half-finished drawing of her sits on an easel, surrounded by the trappings of gracious living: a leather couch, a Persian carpet, and an antique dining table set with flowers and fruit.

The painters of Montparnasse jeered at this vision. No artist could afford such luxury. The studio belonged to journalist and author Sisley Huddleston, the *Times* of London's man in Paris. For most painters, their rented rooms doubled as studios. Others shared space at the art schools along Grande-Chaumière. Purpose-built studios were rare. The building at 31 rue Campagne-Première where Man Ray worked and lived was exceptional, and space in it expensive.

A Studio in Montparnasse, *1926. (C. R. W. Nevinson)*

The influx of foreign artists into Montparnasse sparked a boom in rental accommodations. Buildings of the eighteenth century that had housed two or three families became rooming houses accommodating fifty, but with no improvement in heating or sanitation. Along such streets as rue Delambre, landlords enlarged the windows of attic maids' rooms to create makeshift ateliers with northern light, regarded as the most pure for painting purposes. Their large areas of glass made these uninsulated spaces notoriously chilly. Often the only heat came from a pipe linked to a pot-bellied fuel stove. The scene in the opera *La bohème* where artists burn their books and manuscripts to keep warm was not far from the truth. In 1947, photographers Robert Frank and Elliot Erwitt shared a studio with a sculptor who had acquired a crate of the sort used to ship automobiles. He and his family lived in the box, renting out the remaining space.

Inspired by Montmartre's Bateau Lavoir, formerly a piano factory, speculators converted old workshops and stables into so-called *cités d'artistes*. Where no suitable buildings existed, they constructed them, often cannibalizing trade expositions when their elaborate pavilions were broken up and sold as scrap. In 1889, a builder purchased doors, windows, and other fittings from that year's Exposition Universelle and reassembled them along an alley at

9 rue Campagne-Première to create Cité Taberlet, a village of 128 studios named for the architect who designed it. Modigliani, Whistler, Foujita, Giacometti, Kandinsky, Miró, Ernst, and Friesz all worked there, as did poet Rainer Maria Rilke. His *Notebooks of Malte Laurids Brigge* describes unflatteringly its disproportionate and oddly placed doors, and the mismatched walls, still bearing the marks of former plumbing.

Rue Campagne-Première itself was unpopular, since horse-cab drivers from a nearby depot routinely galloped its length as they headed back to the boulevards. Both cabmen and artists ate inexpensively at Chez Rosalie, a tiny restaurant at 3 rue Campagne-Première, opened in 1906 by Rosalie Robia, a former model of Italian descent who had posed for Odilon Redon and William Bouguereau. Modigliani had his customary stormy relationship with Rosalie, who decorated the café with his drawings, which, during their arguments, conducted in noisy Italian, he would tear from the walls. (The ateliers of Cité Taberlet not demolished in the 1920s have become apartments. Some are fitted out for use by artists, but since real estate in this area now costs about €11,000 a square meter, only the wealthiest can afford them.)

Chez Rosalie, with proprietor Rosalie Robia.

LA RUCHE

2 PASSAGE DANTZIG,
FIFTEENTH ARRONDISSEMENT

Although it lies outside the borders of Montparnasse, the studio complex known as La Ruche is too
significant in the history of art to exclude for reasons of geography.

Around 1900, sculptor Alfred Boucher, made
wealthy by commissions from the king of Greece
and the queen of Romania, decided to share his
good fortune with the quarter by providing in-
expensive work spaces. Because the city had
recently built stockyards and slaughterhouses
nearby, depressing prices, he was able to buy
5,000 square meters of land for a mere franc per
square meter.

Construction began in 1902 with materials
salvaged from the Exposition Universelle of 1900,
in particular an octagonal cast-iron pavilion designed
by Gustav Eiffel for the wine-growers of the Gi-
ronde. Builders created sixty wedge-shaped studios
radiating from a central staircase, a format one artist likened to "an evil Brie cheese" but another to

the cells of a *ruche* or beehive, a comparison that stuck, giving the complex its name.

Boucher, who lived nearby, did his best to create a congenial environment. A gate from the Exposition's Indonesian pavilion provided a stylish entrance, and the British India display the caryatids on either side of the front door. As Boucher sometimes worked on larger commissions in the grounds, picturesque blocks of stone and half-completed figures were scattered about. In 1908, he added a 300-seat theater.

Word spread of the Ruche's low rents and ample space, in particular among artists from eastern Europe, few of whom spoke French. The Russian painter Pinchus Kremegne arrived at the Gare de l'Est with three rubles in his pocket and a single phrase in French: "Passage Dantzig." Once installed, these newcomers communicated only in Polish or Russian. Boucher, who spoke neither, said, "I felt like a hen who had hatched a brood of ducklings." Explosive arguments were common among the tenants, most of them about models, who were supposed to be shared. A tendency for both men and women to become proprietorial ignited violent disputes, often ending with naked women running screaming down the stairs.

Bugs and rats infested the building, the latter so arrogant that, according to Chaim Soutine, one stole the herring he was painting. All the same, the distinguished roster of tenants included Guillaume Apollinaire, Alexander Archipenko, Ossip Zadkine, Moïse Kisling, Marc Chagall, Nina Hamnett, Fernand Léger, Jacques Lipchitz, Max Jacob, Blaise Cendrars, Robert Delaunay, Amedeo Modigliani, Constantin Brâncuși, and Diego Rivera.

Boucher died in 1934. Within a decade, the Ruche was derelict. Threatened with demolition, it was rescued with the support of writers and artists, including Jean-Paul Sartre and Jean Renoir. In 2010, though still occupied by a few working artists, the building and its overgrown grounds looked, in the words of one report, "like a battered old umbrella." (Since then, the Foundation for National Culture, with the assistance of a private fund, has embarked on a program of restoration.)

La Ruche. *(Fernand Léger)*

9

WOMEN AND MAN

THE LOVE LIFE OF MAN RAY

I'm ugly. I have an inexpressive face.
I am small. I'm like all of you!
I wanted to give myself
A little publicity.
MAN RAY

"IT IS SAID," JACQUELINE GODDARD ADMITTED, "THAT
Man Ray started with pornography. And I have seen recently a photograph of Kiki's mouth on Man Ray's private parts." Beyond this, the last survivor of Ray's models, and the one who knew him best, was not prepared to go.

"He was not handsome," said Goddard of the American Surrealist photographer, painter, and filmmaker. "His nose had no opinion and went all over the place. He always seemed to be meditating, and was seldom light-hearted. It was a great pity that he did not smile a lot. That little grin of his changed him altogether."

Strong-featured, with an unruly mane of hair, Goddard, née Borsotti, emerged from the families of Italian artisans who colonized Montparnasse during the building frenzy of the Haussmann years. Although Ray photographed her frequently, they were never—exceptionally for him—lovers. He offered to inscribe one of his photographs to her as "the only model I didn't sleep with" but she demurred; it made his other models sound like whores. After his death, however, his widow, Juliet, signed a lithograph portrait "To Jacqueline, who did not."

That Ray should single out Goddard for her chastity suggests how few Montparnos shared it. If, as Christopher Isherwood confessed, "Berlin meant boys," for Man Ray as for most artists, Paris meant pussy. A surprising success with the women who became his best subjects, he took nudes of his companion Alice Prin, aka Kiki, as well as numerous erotic photographs of other women, both for pleasure and to order. Kiki didn't mind. It aroused her to participate, and to see the reaction when he showed the pictures to prospective clients.

When Henri-Pierre Roché, author of *Jules et Jim*, called to have his portrait taken, Ray, he wrote, showed him "very

Salvador Dali and Man Ray.

moving pictures of lesbians, in eight most luscious poses. I knew one of these beautiful girls. Then, two photos of love-making between a man and a woman." The "beautiful girls" were Surrealist artist Méret Oppenheim and Nusch, wife of priapic poet Paul Éluard. Roché, himself involved in the ménage à trois that inspired his novel *Jules et Jim*, commissioned more of the same. As word got around of Ray's sideline, William Seabrook, voodoo scholar, fetishist, and recreational cannibal, invited him to a dinner during which he displayed a naked girl chained to the stairs. Unblinking, Ray snapped her, as he did a succession of similar posed tableaux on Seabrook's behalf.

Ray came into his own as an eroticist in October 1929 when he featured as both photographer and model in a famous pornographic work. Gathered for their nightly meeting, the Surrealists were unsurprised to hear that the group's Brussels chapter was once again broke. For all his charm, its leader, gallerist Édouard Mesens, was hopeless in business.

Kiki of Montparnasse (Alice Prin) in the 1929 film Galerie des monstres.

"They could do another special issue," suggested Louis Aragon, Breton's tall, soft-spoken lieutenant. Technically Dadaists, the Belgians had recently published a Surrealist number of their magazine *Variétiés*, which sold out.

"Maybe a *special* special issue," mused Breton.

The next afternoon, Aragon headed across the Seine to Montparnasse. It was too early for the cafés, so he knew he would find Man Ray in his studio at 8 rue Val-de-Grâce.

Would he be alone? With Ray, one never knew. It was certain Kiki would not be there. That relationship had ended catastrophically when Henri Broca, publisher of the magazine *Paris-Montparnasse*, convinced her she was sufficiently famous to write her memoirs, which he would publish. She and Broca became lovers. Succumbing to her own hype, she dreamed of a movie career. In more ways than one, Ray looked too small for the star she was about to become.

Aragon entered the little block of apartments in the shade of the seventeenth-century Val-de-Grâce church, with a distant view of the domed Observatory. The stomp of a jazz band became louder as he mounted the stairs and rang a bell which whirred, he said later, "like a desperate cicada."

The music stopped and the door was flung open. Only five feet four inches tall, with a big nose, glaring eyes, heavy brows, and a pronounced widow's peak, Ray reminded Aragon of a bird of prey, interrupted in tearing apart a hapless rabbit.

Saying nothing, Ray stood aside to admit him. Though tiny, the studio was meticulously neat. From its walls, Dogon and Senegalese masks glared down, their features resembling the man who'd hung them.

"Alors, Louis," Ray said in Brooklyn-accented French, *"quoi de neuf à Place Blanche?"*

He'd been working on the photograph of a woman in an evening gown—one of his portrait commissions. Commercial success was one reason for Ray's marginal status among the Surrealists. Breton preferred members of the group to refuse paid employment, since it impeded instinctive creativity. Like his other directions, including one that they avoid "trivial" Montparnasse and no longer patronize brothels, this was more honored in the breach than the observance.

Aragon told Ray about the Belgians, and the idea of a special issue of *Variétés*.

"How 'special,' exactly?" Ray asked.

Aragon laid out the idea hatched with Breton and Benjamin Péret. Each December, postmen, firemen, and garbage collectors went from door to door, selling flimsy "almanacs" as a means of soliciting a Christmas bonus.

Most contained a calendar, a list of saints' feast days, a few jokes, and some pious or decorative images.

It was Aragon's suggestion to parody these humdrum publications by producing a salacious version to benefit Mesens's group. Aragon, Péret, and even Breton had written some raunchy verses to set the tone. He showed Ray a sample.

Ah the little girls who lift their skirts
and diddle themselves in the bushes
or in museums
behind the plaster Apollos
while their mother compares the statue's rod
to her husband's
and sighs . . .

What they needed, Aragon explained, were some illustrations.

Ray slid open the drawer under his worktable and took out a sheaf of prints. They were the photographs he'd shown to Roché of an anonymous couple having sex. The images spilled across the table, swamping the society matron in flesh. Even with faces cropped out, it was obvious Ray and Kiki had posed for them, Ray tripping the shutter with a cable release. In the first, his pale body was sprawled on top of hers. In the second, she had clamped her trade-mark lipsticked mouth around his penis. In the third and fourth, he was penetrating her from front and rear.

Aragon intuited why Ray was offering these images. If Kiki wanted fame, he'd give it to her, with a vengeance. To hate her so much, he mused, Ray must really love her.

The pictures were exactly what Breton needed. The "al-manac," called simply *1929*, contained four groups of verse, named for the seasons, with a Ray photograph prefacing each. Mesens printed 215 copies in Brussels and shipped al-most all of them to Paris, only to have the French *douane* seize the entire shipment at the border. Even so, copies were soon on sale clandestinely in both Paris and Brussels at in-flated prices. (Rare surviving copies sell today for $10,000.)

Obviously someone dropped a dime on *1929*, but who? The Surrealists, to drive up the price? Or Ray, completing his revenge on Kiki?

If Ray meant *1929* to draw a line under that relation-ship, it succeeded. As Kiki embarked on her abortive attempt at stardom, a new woman appeared to replace her. When Lee Miller, an arrogant young American, showed up in Montparnasse and announced she'd come to be his pupil, Ray was ripe for tempting.

Miller was that woman artists both fear and desire: the Eurydice figure; muse and lover, but also destroyer. She posed for him, slept with him, learned from him, and in time betrayed him. Paradoxically, her native puritanism, so unlike Kiki's carnality, inspired some of his best works, including the canvas called *À l'heure de l'Observatoire: Les amoureux* (*Observatory Time: The Lovers*). Like an erotic airship, Miller's lips, crimson with lipstick, both seductive and unattainable, float in the evening sky over Montparnasse. *Soon,* they taunt. *Not just now . . . but soon. . . .*

THE STUDIO OF MAN RAY

31 RUE CAMPAGNE-PREMIÈRE

Mainly remembered today as the place where Man Ray had his home and studio, this building of 1911, containing twenty duplex studio apartments, is distinctive in its own right. Architect André Arfvidson, though French, built in the evolving International style, with elements of art nouveau in the ceramic garlands and masks of the façade, and art deco in the geometric tiles by ceramicist Alexandre Bigot, to which firing at intense heat gave a glass-like glaze.

When he arrived in Paris, Ray shared a work space with Tsuguharu Foujita on rue Delambre, but it was at 31 rue Campagne-Première that he created the images by which he's best known. It is also the home he shared with Kiki, and, later, Lee Miller. Their bed, perched on a mezzanine, overlooked the tiny salon that doubled as his atelier. Film was developed and prints made in a former closet.

Restricted space invited intimacy. For her first session with Ray, Kiki had posed clothed. The next afternoon, she returned to see the results. "Presently she undressed while I sat on the bed with the camera before me," Ray recalled. "When she came out from behind the screen, I motioned for her to come and sit beside me. I put my arms around her, and she did the same, our lips met and we both lay down. No pictures were taken that afternoon."

10

THE QUEEN OF MONTPARNASSE

All I need is an onion, a bit of bread, and a bottle of red, and I will always find somebody to offer me that.
ALICE PRIN, AKA KIKI OF MONTPARNASSE

THE FRANK SEXUALITY AND RAW HUMOR OF ALICE PRIN, aka Kiki, added to an expressive body that fell naturally into the poses required of a model, made her coronation in 1929 as "Queen of Montparnasse" a foregone conclusion. That she should also be provident, abstemious, and discreet demanded too much of this irrepressible and promiscuous woman. Introducing her *Memoirs*, Hemingway wrote that she was "about as close as people get nowadays to being a queen—but that, of course, is very different from being a lady."

As we are attracted to those qualities in a society unlike our own, it was also inevitable that Kiki's spontaneity, vulgarity, shamelessness, honesty, and sex would win over the expatriates. The French were less enthusiastic. While willing to accept foreigners and their alien ways in return for hard currency, they made no such concessions to Frenchwomen. Some cafés refused to serve them unless accompanied by a male. As for going out in public without a hat, a bare-headed woman practically announced herself a prostitute.

Ironically, it was these restrictions that brought together Kiki and Man Ray. In one version of their meeting, Ray, fresh off the boat in 1921, was drinking in a café with Russian artist Marie Vassilieff when Kiki came in selling copies of the pinup magazine *Paris-Montparnasse* and sat down with them. In another, Kiki and a friend, hatless and unescorted, were chatting at a table when the café owner tried to eject them, and Ray intervened.

In whatever way they became acquainted, Ray, Vassilieff, and Kiki left the café together, Alice chattering about her life. At twenty-two, she was tall, with wide hips, small breasts, narrow ankles, and tiny feet. A pointed nose and receding chin were redeemed by electric eyes, which artists liked to elongate, giving her the look of a startled faun. She only sold *Paris-Montparnasse* when modeling work was thin. "I get a couple of sous for the magazine," she said airily, "but the guys in the back room pay me ten francs to show my tits, so I don't do so bad."

She'd just been working in Montmartre, she explained, posing for Maurice Utrillo. An alcoholic, clinically depressed, with a morbid fear of women, he was confined to an upstairs room in the house of his mother, Suzanne Valadon. As part of his therapy, she encouraged him to paint, but only what he could see from his window. Working with a model was something new for him but, Alice continued, when she peeked at the canvas for which she'd posed . . . well, *putain!* Would you believe, he'd done another street scene, with no sign of her in it! Painters! *Dingue*, all of them. Crazy. She'd posed for the best: Soutine, Krohg, Foujita. Though that Foujita . . . did they know he had a real bath in his studio on Delambre, with *hot water*? Half the women in Montparnasse had dropped their knickers in return for a good soak. Not that everyone *wore* knickers, of course. She didn't herself . . . too constricting; besides, it helped when she needed to pee, the *vespasiennes* or pissoirs of Paris being exclusively for male use. . . .

She rambled on. Ray was mesmerized by this free spirit, without inhibitions, so utterly unlike the women of America. In her fragmentary *Souvenirs*, Alice described the rest of that first day.

He told me, "Kiki, don't look at me that way. You
disturb me."

We went to the movies to see Camille. *We*
held hands. Vassilieff, whom I didn't know well,
was there too. She watched us very sympathetically.

Now, he's my lover.

Ray remembered their date as taking place the following day, and the film they saw as *Foolish Wives*, set
on the French Riviera, with Erich von Stroheim as a rake
who preys on the neglected wives of American business-
men. Luring his latest victim to the cottage of a confederate
during a rainstorm, he urges her to "slip out of those wet
things," and courteously turns his back, only to coolly
appraise her body over his shoulder in a pocket mirror. At
this scene, Ray clutched Kiki's hand, and felt a matching
excitement.

Kiki became his model, lover, language tutor, play-
thing, muse, even his hobby—an activity for which the
French have no single word, calling it a *violon d'Ingres*, after
painter Jean-Auguste-Dominique Ingres, who composed
music in his spare time and played the violin. Adding the
f-holes of that instrument to a photograph of Kiki's naked
back, Ray titled the image *Le violon d'Ingres*.

He enjoyed embellishing her face with elaborate makeup in silver and gold, sometimes painting open eyes on her eyelids so that, when she closed them, she appeared to be staring. "Her maquillage was a work of art in itself," wrote John Glassco. "Her eyebrows were completely shaved and replaced by delicate curling lines shaped like the accent on a Spanish ñ. Her eyelashes were tipped with at least a teaspoonful of mascara, and her mouth, painted a deep scarlet that emphasized the sly erotic humor of its contours, blazed against the plaster-white of her cheeks on which a single beauty spot was placed, just under one eye."

Beauty spots had their own language, like much else in a nation where almost everything is conveyed by nuance. The position chosen by Kiki, known as L'Assassinée, signified a killer flirt on the lookout for lovers. It was a symbol the truth of which Ray would soon discover for himself.

SOUVENIRS, KIKI

HENRI BROCA, PARIS, 1929

Unless you count her grave in Montparnasse Cemetery with its modest epitaph "Kiki, 1901–1953, singer, actress, painter, Queen of Montparnasse," Alice Prin's most enduring monument is her so-called autobiography, published in 1929 as *Souvenirs*.

Illustrated with reproductions of the artworks for which she'd posed, as well as a few of her own naive creations, and preceded by praise from Foujita and other former employer/lovers, these scrappy reminiscences were commissioned by Henri Broca, publisher of the magazine *Paris-Montparnasse*. For a few months in 1929 and 1930, she and Broca enjoyed a hot and heavy affair, one incident of which even made the papers. On February 17, 1930, Wambly Bald reported that "two friends, walking along the Boulevard [du Montparnasse], entertained each other and the rest of the promenaders with an endurance kiss. It started near the Falstaff [on rue Delambre] and held until they came in front of the Coupole bar, where they were greeted by the little flower girl. Broca bought a flower, pinned it, and he and Kiki went inside."

The *Souvenirs* were enough of a success for Edward Titus to publish an English version. Translated by Samuel Putnam, with introductions by both Foujita and Hemingway, it was immediately banned by US Customs, guaranteeing a lively clandestine sale and numerous bootleg editions, including one of 1955 that added an extra ten chapters, describing imaginary visits by Kiki to New York, and meetings with the glitterati. By then dead for two years of cocaine and alcohol abuse, she could hardly protest.

11

MAD, BAD, AND DANGEROUS TO KNOW

And is it true? It is not true.
And if it were it wouldn't do
For people such as me and you
Who pretty nearly all day long
Are doing something rather wrong.

HILAIRE BELLOC

IN 1923, 32,000 UNITED STATES CITIZENS LIVED PERMA-
nently in Paris. However, at least two-thirds of them held
residency papers, proof of full-time employment, usually in
banks, import/export companies, and various diplomatic
services. If these Americans visited Montparnasse, it was
only to take some incredulous visitor on a walk through a
part of the city that was, to them, as exotic as Chinatown.
A description of the Café du Dôme in a 1927 guidebook

suggests their scandalized fascination. "You see all the Nuts and all of the Freaks, plain and fancy, broke and affluent, mangy and modish, glassy-eyed and goo-goo-eyed; long-haired and bald-domed; Van Dyke-bearded and pasty-faced; decorous and degenerate; pious and perverted; mademoiselle-ish young men and young-men-ish mademoiselles. Every sort, type, and figured male and female you ever beheld, inside or outside a side-show."

A different but no less unusual crowd gathered at the Dingo Bar on rue Delambre. Its French owner took the plain wooden-floored workingmen's bistro upmarket by renaming it with a corruption of the slang word *dingue* (crazy) and installing ex-boxer Jimmie Charters as barman. Once former Ziegfeld showgirl Angela Martin, known as "Flossie" because of her tangled hairdo, adopted it, the Dingo became an informal clubhouse for expats. Charters wrote:

> *The crowd would begin to drift in any time after noon. Sad individuals with hangovers, or small and quiet sober groups of earnest men and women discussing art, which seemed to be an inexhaustible subject. The hangovers took pick-me-ups and the others sipped their drinks slowly, but by five o'clock the crowd was in full swing. Excited women,*

amorous couples, jittering fairies, gay dogs, over-
serious young men expounding theories, and a few
quiet, observing souls who took it all in and appre-
ciated it.

Most of these people survived on interest from trust funds or allowances sent from home. Any interruption to their hand-to-mouth existence could be catastrophic. When the government halted all foreign currency transactions in 1914 at the outbreak of war, many would have starved had Marie Vassilieff not set up a "canteen" in her home to feed them. Not so fortunate, a group of Chinese students invaded their embassy, looted the larder, and ate the ambassador's lunch.

Typical of American Montparnos, the Hemingways lived on the meager income from Hadley's inheritance, augmented with what Ernest made from journalism. Others found jobs "in the black," teaching English, translating, acting as chauffeurs or, like Kay Boyle, as secretary to a princess and ghosting her memoirs. An attractive person of either sex with a decent backhand, a sound card sense, and one suitcase of good clothes could live year-round as a house guest, though such a life was not without risk. Edith Wharton's 1905 novel *The House of Mirth* detailed the ruin that could befall someone who overplayed her hand, literally in the case of her main character, Lily Bart, who, among other transgressions, loses heavily at bridge.

Americans in Paris would always be outnumbered by other European nationals, particularly by Italians, but also, following the 1917 revolution, by Russians. Unlike rich Americans, who spent their money on pleasure, those czarists who escaped with fortunes intact often used them to furnish their community with hospitals, schools, shops, restaurants, even a cathedral. The less fortunate became factory workers, prized by employers because, hostile to all forms of socialism, they would never, as a matter of principle, go on strike. Others found jobs in hotels and restaurants where they had once been clients. Some drove cabs. As late as the 1930s, France's Union of Russian Cabdrivers had three thousand members.

Not all Russians lived so peacefully. In 1932, a doctor, Pavel Gorgulov, shot and killed France's President Paul Doumer. He claimed to be protesting the plight of his countrymen, but it's more likely he resented his own conviction and deportation for performing abortions. Illegal medicine in all its forms flourished in Paris, led by another Russian, Serge Voronoff, who claimed to rejuvenate men by transplanting the testicle tissue of chimpanzees and baboons into their genitals. Through Marie Vassilieff, his stepdaughter, Voronoff had entrée to artistic circles. Many creative people submitted to his treatments, including author Anatole France, Maurice Girodias, later the publisher of *Lolita*, and also, it's widely believed, Pablo Picasso.

Doumer and Voronoff typified another faction of the expatriate community: the illegal, eccentric, and insane.

At the turn of the century, better-organized and more ruthless criminals from Italy, the Balkans, and eastern Europe squeezed out Paris's native street gangs, the Apaches. At the same time, the anarchist Bonnot Gang streamlined political crime, robbing banks as a form of terrorism and speeding away in automobiles, the first criminals to do so. The Bande à Bonnot inspired the movie serials of Louis Feuillade and pulp novels celebrating super-criminal Fantômas and the avenger Judex. On the inaugural cover of the Fantômas series, he appears as a giant, looming over the city, bloody dagger in hand, but costumed in evening dress, silk hat, and domino, like a boulevardier at a *bal jardin*.

Fortunately, the gangsters and madmen of the quarter were outnumbered by simple eccentrics. As Jimmy Charters wrote. "The most vibrant flavor of personality and internationalism in Montparnasse probably came most insistently from those who had the least inhibitions." In this category, he nominated "Kharis, the tall Hindu with his beautiful white turban, and Granowsky, the 'Jewish cowboy' who wore chaps to ride his bicycle, or the American

Indian who danced on nails, swallowed fire, and stuck pins into his skin in front of the Dôme until the police stopped him." Another client, an English girl, would arrive at the bar in what looked like a dress, only to open it, reveal she was naked, and say in evident surprise, "How silly! I came out in my robe."

One might have thought Charters invented these colorful grotesques, but in fact a painter named Samuel Granowsky did live in Montparnasse during the 1920s. A few photographs, taken around 1925, show him puffing a pipe and wearing a high-crowned black hat that might conceivably be taken for a Stetson. And however improbable it may be for a citizen of the sub-continent to share the name of the ancient Egyptian played by Boris Karloff in *The Mummy*, the existence of this individual is corroborated by Michel Georges-Michel, who wrote of "Kharis, the Hindu, known also as 'The Fakir,' [who] claimed to be living in his six hundredth incarnation and sat from morning to night on the same bench in the café, motionless, breakfasting, lunching and dining on sour milk" (presumably then-exotic yogurt).

Fantômas, *1911*.

THE SURREALIST PRIEST, ERNEST DE GENGENBACH

CAFÉ DU DÔME

Few who hung out at the Café du Dôme could match in flamboyance Ernest de Gengenbach. As a Jesuit seminarian in his early twenties, he'd sneaked away to see a play at the Odéon theater, and fallen in love with actress Régine Flory. After a night spent with her in a *bal jardin*, Gengenbach, reeking of sin, returned to the seminary, where the father superior threw him out.

The lovers never met again. Régine, though only in her twenties, suffered from depression and had already attempted suicide. In 1926, she shot herself in the office of a London impresario whom she'd hoped would revive her stalled career. Hearing the news, Gengenbach contemplated drowning himself, but reconsidered after reading a discussion of suicide in the magazine *La Révolution Surréaliste*. He ambushed André Breton and asked to join the group. Amused that a former seminarian might become part of a movement hostile to religion, Breton introduced him at their next séance, for which Gengenbach wore his long black cassock or *soutane*. Reaction was mixed. Benjamin Péret, so virulently anticlerical that he attacked nuns and priests in the street, slapped his face, but the remaining members were welcoming.

Gengenbach became a regular around Montparnasse cafés, always in his cassock, but with a red carnation pinned to it, and, often, a girl on his lap. Despite this, and notwithstanding writing such provocative books as *Satan in Paris* and *Judas, or The Surrealist Vampire*, he never lost his religious belief, and took regular retreats at the Abbey of Solesmes.

When rumors circulated that he might return to the church, he tried to reassure Breton that he remained an unregenerate sensualist. "It is my custom to go several times a year to rest and recover my spirits with the monks," he explained, "and the Surrealist circle is well aware of my pronounced taste for escapades in monasteries. As for the ecclesiastical habit, I wear it by caprice for the moment because my suit is torn. I also find it affords me certain advantages in initiating sadistic relations with the American women who pick me up in the Bois [de Boulogne] at night. There remains my faith in Christ, cigarettes, and the jazz records I love—*Tea for Two*; *Yearning*—and above all, there remains Surrealism."

Breton wasn't convinced. The Catholic church boasted that, if they had a child for the first seven years, they had him for life—a rule that went double for the Jesuits, its intellectual elite. "M. Gengenbach never really took off his *soutane*," Breton wrote in 1927, "even when he let his mistresses wear it, or sent it out to be re-dyed—something he did as often as he changed his ideas." Gengenbach died in 1979, after periods spent in prison and psychiatric institutions. Breton, who had ejected him from the Surrealists, wrote that "he never succeeded in reconciling, any more than anyone else, the love of a religious order and his love of the profane."

12

CLOSE TO THE BULL

DONALD OGDEN STEWART

Donald Ogden Stewart: Do you speak French?
The author: A little.
Stewart (conspiratorially): Entre nous . . .

WITH HEMINGWAY AND FITZGERALD DOMINATING THE history of expatriate Montparnasse, it's easy to overlook some less famous citizens—even the man who introduced them.

Professional wit, best-selling humorist, and friend of almost everyone, Donald Ogden Stewart survives today mostly in the fictional characters he inspired, among them hard-drinking screenwriter Wylie White in Fitzgerald's unfinished novel *The Last Tycoon*. They worked together at

MGM in 1938. Fitzgerald often showed Stewart the manuscript, and invited comments.

He's also in *The Sun Also Rises*. When Hemingway's alter ego, Jake Barnes, travels to Spain with his lover, Brett Ashley, they're joined by sarcastic, permanently inebriated Bill Gorton. Hemingway's childhood friend Bill Smith, who partly inspired Gorton, agreed that he did possess "a leg as hollow as Lady Brett Ashley's" but insisted "no one man could have drunk as much as Bill Gorton did. [The character] had to be a composite." He was right. The other leg belonged to Don Stewart.

Stewart's humor was no respecter of persons. Edmund Wilson remembered him reeling off a condemnation of their literary friends. "Hemingway is finished. Fitz is finished—he's been getting worse and worse! Dos [Passos] is finished. . . ." In *The Sun Also Rises*, Gorton never stops needling Barnes. "You're an expatriate," he sneers. "You've lost touch with the soil. You get precious. Fake European standards have ruined you. You drink yourself to death. You become obsessed by sex. You spend all your time talking, not working. You're an expatriate, see? You hang around cafés."

Despite these gibes, Stewart insisted, "I really wanted Hemingway to like me." As for Hemingway, he swallowed

Donald Ogden Stewart.

these insults because Stewart wrote for the glossy American magazines, a market he coveted. A 1924 visit to Pamplona, however, offered a chance for payback. After stampeding through the town's narrow lanes, crowded with thrill-seekers, young bulls were corralled in the Plaza de Toros.

The most daring runners entered the ring after them, even though the confined space and shouts of the crowd made the animals even more dangerous.

"Excited, drunk, hot, hungover," Stewart hardly knew what was happening when Hemingway handed him a red cloak and pushed him into the ring. "I found myself standing alone in the midst of an audience of thousands," he wrote, "with the bull glaring at me from a distance of six feet." Fortunately, the horns of the animal had been blunted. It still tossed him twice, but with no injury except to his dignity. "I had been hit by a bull, and it was nothing," he said. "I had shown that I could take it. Ernest clapped me on the back, and I felt as though I had scored a winning touchdown."

Back in Paris, Hemingway wrote a short comic piece called "My Life in the Bull Ring with Donald Ogden Stewart," and sent it to *Vanity Fair*, one of the magazines that published Stewart. At the same time, he asked Stewart to press editor Frank Crowninshield to buy it. Resenting this attempt by a newcomer to invade his territory, Stewart did nothing, and the piece never appeared. Parodying Stewart as Bill Gorton in *The Sun Also Rises*, published two years later, was Hemingway's revenge, compounded in 1937 when he mocked him again as the drunk and burned-out Communist filmmaker John Hollis in *To Have and Have Not*.

Still bruised from Pamplona, Stewart returned to Paris and met up with Scott Fitzgerald, just back from Italy and smarting at the tepid reception of *The Great Gatsby*. They talked, inevitably, of Hemingway. Scott had read his Paris-published books, *Three Stories and Ten Poems* and *in our time*, and recommended his work to his editor, Maxwell Perkins at Scribner's, as "the real thing." Yet he had so far avoided a meeting. Embarrassed by his poor education, Fitzgerald hesitated to approach writers he admired. Nevertheless, he respected Hemingway's work so much that Stewart agreed to introduce them.

Even had Stewart done nothing else, the distinction of introducing Ernest Hemingway to Scott Fitzgerald would have earned him a footnote in literary history, although there are times, reading of this troubled relationship, when it seems everyone would have been better off had they never met. When, after a brief honeymoon period, their friendship soured, Hemingway missed no opportunity to denigrate "poor Scott." The Fitzgerald he describes is a pathetic figure, his talent in decline, ravaged by drink and by Zelda's jealousy and madness.

The more time the men spent together, the more Zelda taunted Scott and his new friend. She found Hemingway "bogus, as phoney as a rubber check," and just "a fairy with hair on his chest." She even resurrected a rumor, concocted by Robert McAlmon, of a gay relationship between them. The accusation stung, since Scott did entertain homoerotic fantasies but never acted on them. They might have made it as lovers, but certainly never as friends. To Ernest, friends were rivals, to be battered in "boxing lessons" and tussles with bulls that left them bruised and subservient. That he never did this with Scott suggests he saw him as a companion of the gentler kind, the true soul mate he never found. In his essay "The Crack-Up," Scott acknowledged the romantic basis of their relationship. "I really loved him," he wrote, "but of course it wore out like a love affair." His surrender came long before. When Zelda claimed Scott's penis was too short to satisfy her, it was Ernest he approached to examine his genitals and reassure him—an incident Hemingway describes with relish in *A Moveable Feast*. One can almost read that chapter, "A Matter of Measurements," as a love story. It's as if Ernest takes Scott in his arms and kisses all his fears away.

(After Stewart's death in 1980, his family found a copy of "My Life in the Bull Ring with Donald Ogden Stewart" among his papers. They suggested *Vanity Fair* might, belatedly, publish it, but Hemingway's heirs refused permission. It later appeared as an appendix to a collection of Hemingway's letters.)

SCOTT FITZGERALD MEETS
ERNEST HEMINGWAY

RUE DELAMBRE, THE FORMER DINGO
AMERICAN BAR AND RESTAURANT,
NOW THE AUBERGE DE VENISE

After working all morning in the Closerie des Lilas, Hemingway sometimes walked down Boulevard du Montparnasse to the intersection with Boulevard Raspail. Since tourists had overrun the Dôme, he preferred to drink at the unassuming Falstaff or Dingo on the thoroughfare behind the boulevard that Strindberg called "dark and quiet rue Delambre, a street that more than any other in the neighborhood can make you miserable."

It was at the Dingo that Don Stewart introduced Hemingway and Fitzgerald early in 1925. Initially, Hem liked the new arrival. "Scott Fitzgerald is living here now and we see quite a lot of him," he wrote to Max Perkins in June. "I have read his *Great Gatsby* and think it is an absolutely first-rate book." He asked Fitzgerald to comment on the first draft of *The Sun Also Rises*. Scott responded with ten pages of suggestions, many of which were adopted.

Sure he had found a friend, Fitzgerald invited Hemingway to accompany him to Lyon to retrieve his car, which had broken down on the way back from Italy. "We had a great trip together," Hemingway told Perkins, "driving his car up from Lyon through the Côte d'Or." To Gertrude Stein, he wrote that they had "a slick drive through Burgundy. He's a peach of a fellow and absolutely first-rate." The worst he has to say of him is that he misspells his name "Hemminway."

The relationship began to sour once Hemingway met Zelda. Recognizing jealousy as the root of her hostility, he employed a characteristic metaphor to describe her—"Hawks don't share." Intuiting her increasingly evident schizophrenia, he mentioned it to Scott, who took no notice. His love encompassed all her defects.

In *A Moveable Feast*, Hemingway recast his relationship with Fitzgerald as that of an established author pestered by a needy admirer. He insisted he didn't read *Gatsby* until after they met, and denied soliciting Scott's advice on *The Sun Also Rises*. His account of their first meeting, replete with suspiciously well-remembered dialogue, further mocked Fitzgerald, depicted as so effusive that Hemingway halts him in mid-flow, chiding him that, in his circle, "praise to the face is open disgrace." The "great trip" to Lyon becomes a catalogue of disasters. Fitzgerald misses the train, leaving Ernest stranded overnight in Lyon. When Scott finally arrives, he's drunk, becomes more so, then collapses with what he fears is pneumonia. To top off the ill-starred expedition, they drive back to Paris in the open car, periodically drenched by rainstorms.

Ernest Hemingway and F. Scott Fitzgerald.

13

A WIT ON THE BLACKLIST

MEETING DONALD OGDEN STEWART

In the 1970s, Stewart and his second wife, Ella Winter, lived in Britain. I visited them often in their mansion overlooking the leafy suburbs of north London. Appropriate to someone best known for his left-wing politics, the house once belonged to Ramsay MacDonald, Britain's first socialist prime minister. Not far away, in Highgate Cemetery, the giant head of Karl Marx atop his tomb stared out over the world he helped create. Winter was the widow of socialist journalist Lincoln Steffens, who famously said, following a visit to the nascent Soviet Union, "I have seen the future, and it *works*." (It was in hopes of impressing Steffens that Hemingway asked Hadley to bring his manuscripts to Switzerland in 1922, only to have them stolen from the train.)

Winter collected modern art, electronic and neon

sculpture. One got used to threading through these cryptic objects, clicking and flashing, that occupied most of the ground floor. Ascending to Stewart's study up the narrow staircase lined with Ben Shahn lithographs was a journey back in time.

At eighty-two, Stewart was a sly old turtle with an impish grin. He had much to smile about. Propping open the study door was a tarnished Oscar, won for turning *The Philadelphia Story*, a play by his friend Philip Barry, into the film that starred Cary Grant, Katharine Hepburn, and James Stewart. Despite some stormy periods, Stewart seemed to have come to a safe and congenial harbor in London. He certainly thought so. "My whole life has been lucky," he beamed. "I was shot in the ass with luck."

Age had not dulled his comic timing. "I can't offer you a drink," he said the first time we met. "They won't allow me alcohol anymore. Only on birthdays."

He let the idea hang in the air just long enough, then inquired, "It isn't *your* birthday, I suppose?"

"No. Sorry."

"Ah well." He nodded, waited a beat, then said, "Perhaps you wouldn't mind writing the date down for me?"

Wit, like rust, never sleeps.

Real life swept Stewart into the spotlight. In 1948, under investigation by the House Un-American Activities

Committee for his Communist affiliations and sure to be blacklisted, even jailed, he and Ella fled to London.

What could have persuaded this genial gentleman, wealthy, feted, the epitome of trivial humor, to join the militant left? The explanation, predictably, had elements of comedy.

In 1936, Stewart made his customary annual trip to London to refresh his wardrobe with some made-to-measure shirts and evening clothes. He also did a little work. The shenanigans of his millionaire friends had made him wonder what might happen if one of them, perhaps a member of the conservative Whitney clan, was inspired by the events then taking place in Spain to turn Communist. It could make, he decided, an amusing play.

"I didn't have any idea of how *tall* Communists were," he said, "so I asked the doorman at Claridge's, where we were staying, if he knew anything about communism. He directed me to a bookshop. I bought John Strachey's *The Coming Struggle for Power* and read it going back on the boat. It was a revelation."

Once the Spanish Civil War broke out, Stewart volunteered his services to the Hollywood left. ("I just said 'Use me!'") He became president of the Hollywood Anti-Nazi League, the American League of Writers, and the Anti-Franco League. ("I loved to be president.") His connections led him naturally into areas where he could apply moral blackmail to the swimming-pool set. Not everyone enjoyed being lectured on social injustice. "I started boring friends about socialism," Stewart said. "I knew I was boring them because I didn't get invited to as many parties as I once had." In London, he'd visited, as usual, Hawes & Curtis, its best formal-wear shop, to order a dozen stiff shirts, a dozen soft shirts, and six bow ties, in expectation of a lively social season. "You know," he told me, somewhat forlornly (and without, I suspect, a grain of truth), "I still have a few of those shirts. They're a bit yellow, but hardly worn."

14

LE DANCING

*Dancing is a perpendicular expression
of a horizontal desire.*
GEORGE BERNARD SHAW

LIKE MOST ASPECTS OF FRENCH CULTURE, DANCING WAS densely encoded with social distinctions and moral taboos. Whether they were socialites in evening dress ascending the grand staircase of the Opéra between lines of saber-carrying imperial guardsmen in silver breastplates, or young men and women eyeing one another across the bare boards of a neighborhood *bal musette* and waiting for the stamp of the accordionist's foot, the French took dancing seriously.

For centuries, what the French called *danses de société*—social dancing—meant such group dances as the quadrille. Men and women lined up opposite one another in multiples of four and performed evolutions not unlike the American square dance. When the waltz, a refinement of an Austrian peasant dance, the Ländler, appeared at the beginning of the nineteenth century, its special scandal wasn't the delirious effect of its whirling motion but the fact that couples danced in one another's arms, not as a group. "No event ever produced so great a sensation in English society as the introduction of the waltz in 1813," remarked one writer, and as late as 1825, *The Oxford English Dictionary* rated waltzing "riotous and indecent."

Anglo-Saxons were accustomed to formal parties where one danced sedately with people one often had known since childhood. They had even gone to the same schools to learn these ritualized steps, as well as the stilted conversation that went with them. ("Do you come here often?") A popular song of 1927, "I've Danced with a Man, Who's Danced with a Girl, Who's Danced with the Prince of Wales," joked that, once the music started, even royalty fell back on cliché:

> *It was simply grand.*
> *He said "Topping band,"*
> *And she said*
> *"Delightful, Sir."*

France had its own take on the Ländler. While the bourgeoisie waltzed, dancers in the *bals musette* developed the java, a jigging variation, double speed, the woman's arms around the man's neck, and his hands often clamped over her buttocks. Café owners who tried to discourage it desisted when the Apaches indicated their approval. Signifiers of class were kept to a minimum. Men retained their hats or caps, and often parked a cigarette in the corner of their mouths. Although masks and costumes were long out of style, incognito was strictly observed, with etiquette stipulating that all parties remain silent as they danced, not even asking each other's name. Complete strangers could dance together, and women could invite men onto the floor with a freedom unknown in conventional society.

This equality ceased the moment dancers stepped back into the real world, but to expatriates, unaware of these implicit codes, the superficial laissez-faire of the dance floor seemed to show the revolution's formula of *liberté, égalité, fraternité* in action. "What appealed to them," wrote Michel Georges-Michel, "was this moral liberty which they knew neither in London nor in any city of free and austere America; this international *kermesse* of la Rotonde, du Dôme, le Parnasse, where, indiscriminately and at any hour, even on Sunday, they could work, drink, play the piano and dance even with girls whom they did not know and who came gladly to make their acquaintance."

Close dancing was the nearest most young people came to sex outside marriage, which made the java hugely popular. The French fiancée of filmmaker Luis Buñuel, impatient with his courtly Spanish manners, introduced him to the Bal Bullier and the pleasures of dancing groin-to-groin. Even during World War I, Paris continued to dance. "The worse the war is, the more depraved civilians become," complained novelist Louis-Ferdinand Céline. "Women

Bals musette, *1931.* (*Louis Bonnotte*)

seem to have a fire in their ass. In time of war, instead of dancing in the parlor, we dance in the cellar."

During the war, new dances invaded France, none so seismic in its effect as the one-step, a variant of the cakewalk, introduced in 1917 by the all-black Marine Corps band of James Reese Europe, former musical director for the dance duo Vernon and Irene Castle, for whom he had originally adapted it.

The French had seen African-American dances before, but only onstage, in minstrel shows. Even after a white duo, the Elks, introduced the cakewalk in 1902, it remained a curiosity until the arrival of Europe's sixty-man traveling show. Europe claimed to have invented the one-step, while also describing it as "the national dance of the negro." There was so little to it—dancers shifted their weight rhythmically from foot to foot, varying the motion with an occasional slide and twirl—that nobody took it seriously until 1917, when Léonid Massine, planning his steps for Erik Satie's ballet *Parade*, sensed that conventional dance would clash with its circus setting and Cubist design, and so incorporated its jigging movements into his choreography to Erik Satie's score.

Had he introduced pole dancing into *Swan Lake*, the effect could not have been more shocking. Among even the most freethinking of spectators, it provoked an ingrained racism. "The one-step, danced in *Parade*!" wrote young composer Francis Poulenc of the premiere. "When *that* began, the audience let loose with boos and applause. For the first time, music hall was invading art-with-a-capital-A." Women in the audience attacked the ballet's designer Jean Cocteau with hatpins. So inflammatory was the effect that sensationalists seeking a new thrill would take a box and have sex during performances.

This collision between American dance and "art-with-a-capital-A" gave birth to France's Jazz Age. The *Revue nègre* of 1925, featuring Josephine Baker, was only one of many jazz shows that filled Parisian theaters for more than a decade. Every liner from New York brought a new dance craze, as well as a fresh African-American ensemble to demonstrate it. Parisians learned the fox-trot, renamed *le fox*, as well as the shimmy, tango, rumba, and Charleston. Since a dance and its performers seldom lasted more than a season, everyone rushed to cash in. When Gilda Gray popularized the shimmy, couturiers created dresses with layers of fringe that fanned out decoratively as the dancer shook her shoulders and breasts. Meanwhile, scouts for the Folies Bergère combed dance schools for an American to train as their own shimmy star. One candidate was an amateur and, at twenty-eight, a little old to make a stage debut, but she wasn't interested anyway, so they crossed Zelda Fitzgerald off their list, leaving her to pursue her doomed attempt at a ballet career.

LAST TANGO IN MONTPARNASSE

LA COUPOLE BALLROOM,
102 BOULEVARD MONTPARNASSE

From the turn of the century, *les dancings*—clubs with a dance floor and a permanent band—proliferated in Paris, initially in Montmartre but increasingly in Montparnasse where premises were more spacious. Once the Rotonde turned its upstairs room into a dance hall and hotels and cabarets around Gare Montparnasse and rue de la Gaîté followed suit, the entrepreneurs building La Coupole knew a ballroom was essential.

The tango arrived in Europe from the Argentine via Marseilles. By 1909, it was already being danced, if rather stiffly, in Montmartre. In 1921, a virtuoso screen performance by former taxi dancer Rudolph Valentino in *The Four Horsemen of the Apocalypse* guaranteed his stardom and that of the dance. By the time La Coupole's dance hall opened in 1928, the tango was the most popular dance in Europe, nowhere more so than in Paris.

French dancers lost no time in giving it their distinctive twist. Out went the macho strut of Buenos

Aires, where pimps sometimes danced it together in brothels. Replacing it was something slinkier, a ballet of seduction, the man strutting, the woman swooning in his arms. Couturiers rushed out dresses in "tulip" style, with skirts of overlapping panels that left the legs free for the tango's long loping steps, its swerves and kicks. Serious dancers discarded conventional hats, particularly those with horizontal feathers, which could swipe a partner across the face. They preserved propriety by adopting the forehead band made popular by Irene Castle, sometimes with the addition of a modest plume. Corsets were abandoned, or replaced by more elastic "foundation garments." Paris corsetiere Madame Augustine Thomas actually called her creation Le Tango, and promised firm support with maximum flexibility.

At La Coupole, the *orquesta típica* of Argentinean Juan Bautista Deambroggio, known as "Bachicha" ("wop" or "dago" in the period's racist slang), and his partner Eduardo Bianco played authentic tangos with the traditional instrumentation of two violins, flute, piano, double bass, and the Argentinean accordion known as a *bandoneón*. Their gaucho outfits, complete with the baggy pants so dashing on Valentino, looked a little ridiculous, but *tango-manes*, mesmerized by the music, prowled and swiveled across the floor as if possessed by Terpsichore, the Muse of dance herself.

It was left to Kees van Dongen to create the image that epitomized the tango craze. He began *The Tango of the Archangel* in 1922 and refined it for almost a decade, adding layer upon layer of delirium.

Through a night sky filled with clouds, a couple glide in a tango so intense they might almost be one person. Except for silk stockings, garters, high-heeled shoes, and a jeweled diadem, she's nude. He, in contrast, is formal in black, except for a pair of giant feathered wings folded over his back. While her face, as naked as her body, is flushed with arousal, his is unseen, buried in the hollow of her throat, while one leg thrusts imperiously between her thighs. If this is an angel, it is clearly one of the fallen.

Apollinaire dismissed van Dongen as an artist of "opium, ambergris [the pungent secretion of whales, used in perfume] and eroticism." Later writers suggested the painting didn't belong in an art museum at all but would have been more appropriate as the drop curtain for a Buenos Aires theater specializing in sexual exhibitions. Neither was entirely wrong. Yet arguably these are the very tendencies that qualified van Dongen to confect a vision of the tango that truly reflected Montparnasse: vice and style, inextricably entwined.

Attempting to sum up the lure of the tango, illustrator Georges Gourat, aka Sem, entangled himself in mixed metaphors, but nevertheless came close to capturing in words the synthesis of carnality and exaltation.

> The tango of Paris, you see, is the skin of a stinking animal arriving from the depths of Siberia, soiled and smelly, which the magic hands of furriers have made into a precious sable to caress the perfumed and fragile shoulders of Parisiennes. The tango of Paris is the Argentinean tango without the nicotine. It is a black and juicy Havana, metamorphosed into a slim golden cigarette.

Tango of the Archangel, *1922. (Kees van Dongen)*

15

THE SOUND OF
ONE HAND READING

*He is fiddling while Rome is burning, and, unlike
the enormous majority of people who do this,
fiddling with his face towards the flames.*
GEORGE ORWELL ON HENRY MILLER

"I WANT YOU IN MY MOVIE," NEIL PEARSON SAID.

Though Gore Vidal claimed never to miss a chance to have sex or appear on television, I've learned to pause before leaping into either situation. And while Neil is an actor of impressive range who has played Pinter, Orton, and Stoppard onstage and numerous roles in films and television, some of his recent screen appearances have been as Renée Zellweger's boss in *Bridget Jones's Diary* and its sequels: movies noted for putting performers in uncomfortable situations.

Remembering a scene from the first of the series, I asked, "Will I have to run around in the snow wearing leopard-print underwear?"

"Maybe later," he said. "What I mostly need you to do is talk about dirty books."

Actors are generally book people. Survival rations for the mind, books divert them in those long waits between scenes and, during afternoons in provincial hotel rooms, are more effective than alcohol at placating the black dog of depression. That said, most drop the book as soon as the curtain goes up or the director calls "Action!" Not so Neil, who is a collector and dealer with a scholarly interest in literature of the 1920s and 1930s, in particular what are known in the shorthand of the trade as DBs—dirty books.

Until Denmark legalized pornography in 1969, the gold standard in erotica was signified by the phrase "Published in Paris." This wasn't entirely because of the city's reputation for sensual gratification, though that came into it. Of more significance was the French law on obscenity, which only covered works in French. A British editor of racy literature could print books in Paris and even advertise they'd been produced there, while his French opposite number had to claim his publications came from Constantinople, Amsterdam, Athens, Benares, Moscow, even London—anywhere but France.

As the printer of an obscene book could be prosecuted along with its writer and publisher, most were cautious, even about books in other languages. When Sylvia Beach offered to publish James Joyce's *Ulysses*, she sent the manuscript to Maurice Darantière in Dijon, hoping its ribaldry would mean nothing to his typesetters. It didn't—but neither did any number of perfectly innocent English words. It took eight printings to weed out the typographical errors.

Some of the most unusual DBs were produced by Jack Kahane, a Briton who moved to Paris after World War I, founded the Obelisk Press, and published titles by, among others, James Joyce, Lawrence Durrell, D. H. Lawrence, Anaïs Nin, and Henry Miller. I didn't fully appreciate the degree of Neil's fascination with Kahane until he asked to spend some time with the Obelisk books in my collection. "Don't tell anyone," he said, "but I'm doing a bibliography."

Called simply *Obelisk*, this 500-page labor of love not only lists and anatomizes every Kahane book but includes biographies of all his authors. These often sulfurous profiles are the book's real meat. In Neil's racy exposition, a dirty dozen or two of good, bad, and truly awful writers, brothers and sisters to the Sunday painters who crowded the schools of rue de la Grande-Chaumière, are resurrected to once again walk the streets of Montparnasse.

Having dragged them into the light, Neil, with relish,

dispatches the less talented back to oblivion. Nadejda de Bragança might have been "moneyed, titled, and beautiful" but her *Poems for Music* are "adolescent, hormonally over-heated maunderings." Frank Harris's *My Life and Loves*, a best-seller for Kahane, is "a deranged monument to egotism" written by "a bumptious loudmouth, a man who was little more than vanity wrapped in skin." He's a little kinder to the author of *Dark Refuge*, Charles Beadle, "an assiduous, evangelical user of opium and hashish," and positively complimentary about the gay novel *The Young and Evil* by Charles Henri Ford and Parker Tyler. Despite a text so obscure that "maiden aunts and masturbators alike would be confounded," he applauds the book's frankness, and Kahane's courage in publishing it. "The characters wear makeup and women's clothes, they have sex with strangers, they sleep three in a bed—and they're *happy*." He has less time for Kahane's most gifted author, James Joyce: "a sponger and parasite, an atrocious abuser of friendships who happened to be the literary genius of the twentieth century."

The jewel in the tarnished crown of the Obelisk Press was Henry Miller's 1934 *Tropic of Cancer*, a blustering memoir of unbuttoned days roistering around Paris with his confederate Alfred Perlès. Even Ezra Pound, not given to hyperbole, welcomed "an unprintable book that is fit to read."

In one of those coincidences typical of Paris, Neil had hardly returned to London after shooting his film before another friend, Béatrice Commengé, translator of more than a dozen books by Anaïs Nin, Miller's lover, and the dedicatee of *Tropic of Cancer*, showed me some letters written to her by Nin and Miller during the 1970s. "Anaïs Nin is slowly dying," Miller wrote. "I don't know if you will be able to see her. You should go to see Alf [Perlès] in the Thos. Hardy country of England. Of course he would like to know if you are *jolie* [i.e., pretty]. He adores women as he does flowers. A delightful rogue."

In contrast to Nin's spidery hand, Miller's exuberant scrawl spoke of a life lived as vigorously at eighty as when he wrote *Tropic of Cancer* more than forty years earlier. Soon after writing to Béatrice, he launched an epic 1,500-letter correspondence with a voluptuous twenty-year-old Floridian named Brenda Venus. "To love at the end of one's life is something special," he told her. "Few women can inspire that sort of love. To wake up with the words of love on one's lips—what bliss! Just to say 'Brenda' puts me in ecstasy."

Kahane died in 1939. After the war, his son, Maurice Girodias, relaunched the business as the Olympia Press.

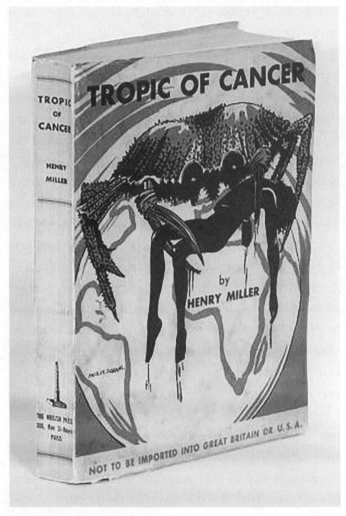

First edition of Henry Miller's Tropic of Cancer.

Always ready to pay a meager $500 for a passably well-written and imaginative DB, he became the employer of last resort for struggling expatriates. Most had never written such material before, nor ever would again. Pseudonyms were standard. As "Count Palmiro Vicarion," British poet Christopher Logue wrote the novel *Lust* and compiled a collection of erotic limericks. In later life, he would grudgingly sign copies of these books, but only if one hid the covers. To translate the Marquis de Sade, Austryn Wainhouse created an Italian version of his name, "Pieralessandro Casavini." Scots novelist Alexander Trocchi became "Frances Lengel," the American poet Jack Gilbert was "Tor Kung," and, as "Maxwell Kenton," Mason Hoffenberg collaborated with Terry Southern, later to script *Easy Rider* and *Dr. Strangelove*, on *Candy*, an erotic female version of Voltaire's *Candide* that became an international best seller.

"He published everything," recalled Hoffenberg of Girodias. "He had this beautiful racket going. Paris was the only place you could print dirty books in English. All the tourists and soldiers bought them, and you got a lot of mail orders from Moscow and Tokyo. Most of the books were terrible." Most, but not all. Like his father, Girodias nursed immortal as well as immoral longings. Many readers first encountered Samuel Beckett, William Burroughs, Jean

Genet, and J. P. Donleavy inside Olympia's sage-green covers. His literary ambitions irritated his core clientele, who only wanted honest porn. "You're giving yourself a bad name," one chided him. Reputable writers were no happier. Vladimir Nabokov, whose *Lolita* Girodias published when no one else would, commented sourly that "alongside talented, albeit immodest, literary works, the publisher gained his main income from vulgar little books that he commissioned from meretricious nonentities, books of exactly the same nature as the pictures hawked on dark corners of a nun with a Saint Bernard, or a sailor with a sailor."

Irish author J. P. Donleavy proved the undoing of Olympia. Having paid a pittance for his novel *The Ginger Man*, Girodias produced numerous editions, paying Donleavy little or nothing. The writer only retrieved his copyright when the company went bankrupt and was sold at auction to pay taxes. Donleavy bought it—more in sorrow than in anger, according to other Girodias veterans. "Basically, Maurice and Donleavy liked each other," said one, "and through the lawsuits that kept them together seems to run a thread of mutually unrequited love. Twenty-five years later, Donleavy was asking, 'What did he say about me?'"

AN UNPRINTABLE BOOK
THAT'S FIT TO READ

TROPIC OF CANCER, AVAILABLE AT ALL GOOD BOOKSTORES

Anaïs Nin, whose banker husband left her free to pursue her affairs, including one with Henry Miller, financed *Tropic of Cancer* with money borrowed from yet another lover, her analyst Otto Rank. Kahane wasted none of it on production. The paper was one step away from newsprint and the cover, showing a giant crab carrying the body of a naked woman, was drawn, with colossal indifference to the actual content, by Maurice, his fifteen-year-old son. Printed in lots of 500 and dribbled into the market through a network of drifters and petty thieves who hawked copies around the tourist cafés, the book quickly won an underground reputation that swelled as, one by one, the nations of the English-speaking world slammed their doors on it.

For my part in his film, Neil asked me to meet him opposite La Coupole and explain the significance of the quarter at the time *Tropic of Cancer* was published. Shivering on the draftiest street corner in Montparnasse, I stared longingly into the cafe's cozy interior. Later, the scene shifted to our apartment, where Neil leafed through a first edition of *Tropic*. Then, looking earnestly into the camera and speaking in a slow, deliberate voice, he read a passage aloud.

> *O Tania, where now is that warm cunt of yours, those fat, heavy garters, those soft, bulging thighs? There is a bone in my prick six inches long. I will ream out every wrinkle in your cunt, Tania, big with seed. I will send you home to your Sylvester with an ache in your belly and your womb turned inside out. Your Sylvester! Yes, he knows how to build a fire, but I know how to inflame a cunt. I shoot hot bolts into you, Tania, I make your ovaries incandescent.*

Hearing the words in his professionally nuanced delivery brought them to life as never before. For the first time, I experienced some of the shock Miller hoped to incite. This was why the likes of Miller, Joyce, and Hemingway came to Paris—to write not as dictated by a publisher or even a reading public but simply out of their own imagination.

"A year ago, six months ago," Miller wrote, "I thought that I was an artist. I no longer *think* about it—I *am*. Everything that was literature has fallen from me. There are no more books to be written, thank God. This then? This is not a book. This is libel, slander, defamation of character. This is not a book in the ordinary sense of the word. No, this is a prolonged insult, a gob of spit in the face of Art, a kick in the pants to God, Man, Destiny, Time, Love, Beauty . . . what you will."

✳ ·16· ✳

A DEPOT NAMED DESIRE

*France in my mind [is] irregularly squarish, and a
line of railway tracks, like a zipper, speeding open to
the south, to Marseilles, to Nice and the Côte d'Azur.*
SYLVIA PLATH

SINCE 1969, THE TOUR MAINE-MONTPARNASSE, FIFTY-
nine floors of featureless black glass, has loomed over the
southern skyline of Paris like some monstrous Godzilla.
Its selection as the world's second-ugliest building, rivaled
only by Boston City Hall, did have one positive result. Two
years after the tower's completion, Paris reaffirmed its allegiance to the city plan of Baron Haussmann and banned all
buildings of more than seven stories.

At the foot of the tower is the Montparnasse railway
terminal. Opened in 1840 as the Gare de l'Ouest, rebuilt
in 1852, then again in 1969, the depot is one of two stations

serving the Atlantic and Mediterranean coasts of France. Not for it, however, such luxury passenger services as the all-first-class Blue Train that departed nightly for the Côte d'Azur, Monaco, and the Italian Riviera. That left from the Gare de Lyon, on the other side of the Seine. Waiting to board its blue steel cars, Winston Churchill, Coco Chanel, Charlie Chaplin, Agatha Christie, and Cole Porter (who booked a whole car, with bedrooms for himself and wife, as well as space for servants) could relax with a glass of champagne in the station buffet, a monument to the *belle époque* in marble, gilt, and brass, decorated with paintings of exotic destinations.

The Gare Montparnasse offered no such luxury. Quite the reverse, its unromantic facilities reflected the businesslike nature of the areas it served. In summer, stalls on the concourse sold grapes from the Médoc and, in winter, oysters from Oléron. Farmers looking to publicize their produce brought picturesquely costumed locals up from the country to show off their prize pigs. Shops stocked everything the traveler might need, from umbrellas to shoelaces. During the 1920s, a bearded old gentleman sold toys and candy from such a stall, unrecognized by almost everyone as cinema pioneer Georges Méliès, set up in this small business on the charity of his few admirers in the industry.

Many Montparnasse artists perceived the station as

Grape seller, Gare Montparnasse, 1920s.

a door opening on the exotic. It was through this station that fellow exiles arrived from Spain and even Africa. With them came the products of their fields and orchards, some barely known to northern Europe in those days before refrigerated shipping. After World War II, the end of austerity was marked by the appearance of tropical fruit in Paris shops, most of it shipped through Gare Montparnasse. The first bananas and pineapples arrived in the luggage of émigrés from France's African colonies, Morocco, Algeria, and Senegal, who sold them in the streets. Italian Surrealist Giorgio de Chirico painted the station repeatedly. *Le rêve transformé* (*The Transformed Dream*) and *Gare Montparnasse: The Melancholy of Departure* (1913 and 1914, respectively) juxtaposed empty platforms and esplanades with bunches of bananas, green or ripe, to signify desire thwarted or satisfied.

Among the hotels, cafés, and cabarets clustered around the depot and along Boulevard Edgar Quinet and rue de la Gaîté, many catered to an Afro-French clientele. One nightclub in particular became a focus of African social life. During the week, 33 rue Blomet, formerly a farmhouse, sold cigarettes and cigars. A large back room was used as an office by Jean Rézard des Wouves, a West Indian politician. Between Friday and Tuesday, however, furniture was cleared away, a bar set up, and the

The Melancholy of Departure, *1914. (Giorgio de Chirico)*

Bal Nègre, an early example of the "pop-up," opened for business.

"In one of the most romantic districts of Paris," wrote Robert Desnos, "where every gate hides a leafy garden, an oriental cabaret has taken root. A real black cabaret where everything is black, including the musicians and dancers, and where one can, on Saturday and Sundays, escape from the atmosphere of Paris into a dream of Martinique or Guadeloupe."

The bar served only *punch*, a potent rum concoction

sweetened with sugarcane and spiced with ginger and cloves, and the air was thick with smoke from kief, a powdered cannabis from north Africa. Montparnos and such occasional celebrity visitors as Maurice Chevalier and his lover Mistinguett were outnumbered by flashily dressed factory workers from North Africa or the West Indies, often dancing with those bourgeois Frenchwomen with a taste for such men who patronized multiracial clubs like Montmartre's Le Paradis.

The Bal Nègre paralleled such New York cabarets as the Cotton Club, with one important difference. In Harlem, black artists performed for an all-white audience. On rue Blomet, the races mingled in equality, both on and off stage. When mixed-race Josephine Baker appeared there, her old companion from the *Revue nègre*, Sidney Bechet, led the band, while a former lover, Paul Colin, who was white, designed the poster. Some visitors were scandalized. A guidebook indignantly described "black men dancing with French girls. Black women dancing with white men. Men dancing with their hats on. Black man walks about the tables trying to get a white partner. He gets one. She dances with both arms around his neck."

Closed during the Nazi occupation, the Bal Nègre revived in the 1940s as part of the postwar enthusiasm for everything American. Instead of show business stars, the new clientele were intellectuals from Saint-Germain-des-Prés, including Boris Vian, Albert Camus, Jacques Prévert, Juliette Gréco, even Jean-Paul Sartre and Simone de Beauvoir, who wrote about it in her memoirs.

> *On Sunday evenings, we abandoned the bitter elegance of skepticism to enjoy the magnificent animalism of the blacks on rue Blomet. At that time, very few whites mixed with the black crowd; even fewer ventured onto the dance floor. Compared to the supple Africans and quivering West Indians, the stiffness of those who did was embarrassing. It was worse when they tried to imitate the blacks; they looked like hysterics in a trance. I enjoyed watching the dancers; I drank some punch; the noise, the smoke, the vapors of alcohol, the violent rhythms of the band numbed me. Through this mist, I saw handsome and happy faces. My heart beat faster as the dancing mounted to a climax. In that final ecstatic unleashing of physical energy, I felt something like my own passion for life.*

GARE MONTPARNASSE

THE CRASH OF '95

Gare Montparnasse achieved a rare moment of international fame on October 22, 1895. As the Granville–Paris Express pulled in at 4 p.m., thirteen minutes late, the driver of locomotive 721, Guillaume-Marie Pellerin, a nineteen-year veteran with Chemins de Fer de l'Ouest, realized that, in an attempt to make up time, he'd been traveling too fast. He signaled the guard in the last van, Albert Mariette, to hit the emergency brakes.

Seeking a scapegoat for what followed, the company would blame the Westinghouse compressed-air brakes with which the train was fitted. Unlike manual brakes, which slowed the train gradually, the Westinghouse system, intended for emergencies, locked the wheels. The guard controlled both, and should have applied them as soon as the driver signaled. However, he did nothing until it was too late.

Watched by horrified travelers, the train, comprising a locomotive, three goods vans, a mail van, and six passenger coaches, exploded through the buffers and stone abutment marking the end of the line. Plowing through a hundred feet of asphalt as if it were cheese, it demolished a two-foot-thick brick wall and rumbled across a terrace toward the windows overlooking Place de Rennes. Bursting through the glass, the locomotive teetered on the edge for a few seconds, then tipped forward to bury its nose in the forecourt thirty-three feet below. One hundred and thirty-one passengers climbed out, astonished to find themselves in one piece. At a newsstand down on Place de Rennes, Marie-Augustine Aguilard was not so lucky. Standing in for her husband while he collected the afternoon papers, she was crushed to death by masonry from the façade.

It took two days to remove Engine 721. As long as it remained in place, crowds came to gawk and photographers to take pictures, which traveled around the world. After a team of fourteen horses failed to lift it, ten men operating a 250-ton winch lowered the locomotive to the ground.

In the inquiry that followed, Chemins de Fer de l'Ouest and its employees escaped lightly. The guard said he had been too busy with paperwork to hear the warning, but it was assumed he'd been drowsing. He was fined twenty-five francs, the equivalent of two weeks' wages. Driver Pellerin was fined fifty francs, and sentenced to two months in prison, suspended. Neither the rolling stock nor the locomotive were badly damaged. Only two passengers were slightly hurt. As for the unfortunate Madame Aguilard, the company paid for her funeral and gave her husband and two children a lifetime pension.

To the embarrassment of the railroad, an almost identical accident took place five years later in the same station and for the same reason. On Monday, September 24, 1900, the 7:28 a.m. train from Versailles, packed with 1,200 commuters, arrived thirteen minutes late and failed to stop. It smashed through the buffers and would have followed Engine 721 into Place de Rennes but for a wide staircase opposite the end of the platform, down which the locomotive plunged. Only 20 passengers were slightly hurt. Once again, technology was blamed and human error excused. "How often terrible accidents are caused by a leak of air in the brakes," a journalist lamented, "the inattention of a weary mechanic, or a misunderstanding."

Gare Montparnasse, October 22, 1895.

17

THE FIFTH-BEST TARTARE
IN PARIS

All men eat, but the man of
intelligence knows how to eat.
JEAN ANTHELME BRILLAT-SAVARIN

"WILL THERE BE FOOD IN THIS BOOK?" OUR DAUGHTER Louise asked. "Did people eat in those days?"

"Of course."

"Then why don't they talk about it? There's lots of drinking—but eating? Not so much."

I had to agree. Whatever reason people had for coming to Montparnasse, it wasn't the food. But a writer must stick up for His People. So I said, "There's Hemingway's favorite lunch at Brasserie Lipp—*cervelas* sausage on cold potato salad. He writes about that."

"One dish? Not exactly a feast, moveable or otherwise."

"What about Alice B. Toklas and her cookbook?"

"But she wrote that much later, didn't she? In her seventies? And didn't you tell me she never cooked half those things? I can believe it. Remember that Josephine Baker chocolate pudding you cooked?" She made a face.

I thought the real low point was her recipe for seafood-stuffed chicken, complete with the feet, but this was no time to concede that *The Alice B. Toklas Cookbook* belonged in the library, not the kitchen. Foreseeing a rout, I ran for cover. "Don't you have something to do?"

Conscious she'd struck a nerve, she picked up her bag. "Let me know if you need any restaurant tips."

I thought about what she said. The French sense of eating as an affirmation of culture wasn't shared by the expats. They just wanted meat and potatoes, and plenty of both. Of the local diet, they knew mainly that the French ate things no right-thinking person would touch. Snails. Chicken gizzards. Smelly cheese. Garlic. Tourist guides of the time articulated this distaste. *How to Be Happy on the Riviera*, published in 1927, spends pages disparaging the food. "Too much butter is used," the writer complains. "Too many dishes which would otherwise be palatable [are] spoiled by highly flavored sauces." Beef is "on the tough side," mutton "awful," white asparagus "bitter," and other boiled vegetables "a ghastly job." As for fresh seafood, he calls fried sardines "rather a disappointment," and continues smugly, "There can be no doubt that providence intended sardines to be tinned."

Of garlic, there's no mention. How would he have reacted to eating with the novelist Colette? A typical lunch at her home near Saint-Tropez began, according to her husband, with "a crust of bread dipped in olive oil, lavishly rubbed in garlic and sprinkled with coarse salt. Cooked garlic seasoned every dish, and in addition, throughout the whole meal, Colette ate raw cloves of it as if they had been almonds. Lunch consisted of Provençal dishes only: green melons, *anchoïade* [anchovies pounded with garlic, oil, and vinegar, and served as a dip with raw vegetables], stuffed *rascasse* [a fish], rice with *favouilles* [small green crabs], *bouillabaisse* [Provençal fish stew] and *aïoli* [garlic mayonnaise]."

Julian Street's 1929 *Where Paris Dines* tries to be even-handed about the transatlantic diet, even listing a few of Paris's American-style restaurants, most of them owned by or employing African-Americans who stayed on after the war. "The citizen of the United States," he writes, "oppressed by a nostalgia, may now soothe himself with dishes ranging from cornflakes and shredded wheat to chicken Maryland, waffles, sundaes, and soda water"—none of which, obviously, Street found even remotely tempting. Americans asking for such things in an ordinary French restaurant risked being shown the door. The chef at Voisin, one of the temples of gastronomy, refused an American lady's request for a plain green salad without dressing. To collude in such an abomination would insult his expertise. Something similar happens in the film *Ninotchka* when Greta Garbo as a Russian commissar in Paris orders "raw beets and carrots" for her lunch. "Madame," says the café owner, with commendable restraint, "this is a restaurant, not a meadow."

Approaching the question from a different direction, I checked up on where the Montparnos might have eaten. The *crèmeries* along rue de la Grande-Chaumière were mentioned, and Chez Rosalie on rue Campagne-Première, but mainly because they were cheap, or offered credit. All were long gone, of course. As for haute cuisine, it was vanishingly rare in Montparnasse. The best restaurants were on the Right Bank, clustered around the Opéra, or along rue Faubourg du Saint-Honoré and the Champs-Élysées. The few on the Left Bank, notably the Tour d'Argent and Lapérouse, clung to the Seine. People venturing any farther up the slope were generally seeking the satisfaction of other appetites. Even today, Montparnasse is not a district to which one goes in search of good food. A few places make it into the most popular restaurant guide, the Gault & Millau, but when a Left Bank establishment displays a decal on its window designating it as the choice of some food guide, it's generally for one of the down-market compendia I think of as *Eat Good Cheap*.

So on what basis could one rate the cuisine of modern Montparnasse? I was still mulling the problem when Louise provided the answer. Her SMS was brief.

8 @ Charivari Mpnasse 5th best tartare in
Paris yum (:

The fifth-best tartare in Paris? If true, it was certainly tempting.

Nothing brings meat eaters closer to pure enjoyment than *boeuf tartare*. It's the French equivalent of the American T-bone or sirloin and the British roast beef: the standard by which carnivores measure quality. The basic recipe is simple: Take a piece of lean steak, chop it finely, ideally with knives, add a minimum of seasoning, and serve it with, at most, a little salad and a few *frites*.

Or that, at least, is how it should be. Too many restaurants buy their tartare in vacuum-packed portions, prechopped. Others use cheaper cuts of fresh meat and mince them, a process that tears, stretches, and tangles the fibers.

The worst option is the food processor, from the blades of which the meat emerges as a gluey pink paste, a glob of which, naked on a plate, has all the appeal of a foot that has gone to sleep.

Food guru M. F. K. Fisher, while finding all forms of tartare "slightly barbaric," spoke up for the classic recipe: chopped meat, enhanced with, at most, fresh parsley or chives, an egg yolk, salt, pepper, and a little olive oil. "Keep it from the eager exhibitionism of the waiter," she urged—still good advice, but not respected by the chefs at such places as La Coupole. There they serve the patty surrounded by small heaps of chopped onion, parsley, pickled cucumber, and capers, with a raw egg yolk squatting on top, sometimes nestled in half an eggshell. The waiter asks if you wish it "prepared." If you do, he disappears, to return with all the additions mixed in, and carrying bottles of Worcestershire sauce, mustard, ketchup, and Tabasco, in case you feel it needs even more seasoning.

Enthusiasts seek the perfect tartare as obsessively as Ahab pursued Moby Dick. Each time a magazine like *Le Nouvel Observateur* or *Le Figaro* announced a superior new source, they flock to check it out. One review, throbbing with appetite, rated a small bistro in Montparnasse as "the nirvana of tartare." He promised "a hefty serving of 350 grams ('We do not weigh it, monsieur!'), finely but not copiously seasoned, with whole capers in sufficiently small numbers to avoid acidity. This is the art of seasoning: to avoid the 'big guns' but add it by the millimeter and leave the meat enough time to recover. And the chopping? I know what you think, purists. It's not a real tartare unless you chop it with knives! You're wrong. Pleasure and taste can hide anywhere, and here, believe me, they jump in your face, knives or no knives."

The review was sufficiently enthusiastic to intrigue me. Small and modern, the restaurant occupied a corner on an otherwise unremarkable street. Chalked on its *ardoise* were the usual suspects of bistro cuisine: *boudin noir*, *blanquette de veau*, *soupe au poisson*—and *bœuf tartare*. It arrived already prepared, accompanied by salad and frites. The *frites*, thick cut, well browned, but not crisp, were happily remote from the shriveled slivers served at burger joints. The tartare itself was just as uncompromising. I tasted finely chopped onion and whole capers, but, aside from the egg yolk, salt, and pepper, nothing else. Even if the meat was minced, not chopped, the satisfaction of pure beef was unimpaired. Everything was *comme il faut*: as it should be.

But perfect? Who knew? There was no absolute with which to compare it. Where did the dish come from anyway? Unlike most French food, it had no regional associations. Why was it even called "tartare"?

No two authorities agreed. One blamed the Asian Tartars who invaded Europe in the fourteenth and fifteenth centuries. Supposedly they gnawed raw meat as they rode, too busy looting and pillaging to stop and cook it. Another suggested they put meat under their saddle in the morning so that the pounding of the day's riding, plus the effect of the animal's sweat, would tenderize it by nightfall. I could well believe this, but was in no hurry to discover for myself.

Someone else thought it took its name from *sauce tartare*, a mixture of mayonnaise, chopped onion, capers, and pickles. It traditionally accompanied fish, not meat—and yet . . . could it be just coincidence they shared some ingredients—pickles, capers, onion?

I dug further, looking for the ur-recipe that marked the birthplace of this icon of French cuisine. It didn't take long. The dish appeared for the first time in the 1921 edition of Georges Auguste Escoffier's bible of gastronomy, *Le guide culinaire*. Back then, however, it wasn't called steak tartare but *steak à l'américaine*—steak American-style.

Could it be that steak tartare came to France with entirely different foreign invaders: not Tartars but Americans? It wasn't such an outlandish idea. Deconstructed, *bœuf tartare* was just a hamburger—admittedly somewhat underdone. I could almost reconstruct the moment of invention. 1919. Two doughboys in a bistro, probably drunk, are explaining to a waiter that they want a hamburger—something invented in Chicago in 1904, and still totally unknown in France. Having described the ingredients—minced beef, onion, pickle—they would have been astonished to be served all these, just differently arranged.

"No, no, we said rare, not raw. . . ."

But meanwhile, in the kitchen, the chef was tasting it, and saying, "Y'know, these Americans are crazy, but this isn't half bad."

I put this theory to my friend Boris as we walked up rue Bréa one evening a few days later, heading for its intersection with Boulevard Raspail and Boulevard du Montparnasse, and a rendezvous with, reputedly, the fifth-best tartare in Paris.

Boris looked even more than usually morose, his thick mustache drooping like damp seaweed. The responsibility of being a gastronome, one of those rare individuals responsible for the maintenance of standards in French food, weighed heavily on his thin shoulders.

"Do you think it's possible?" I asked.

"That Americans invented the tartare?" he said. "Who knows? They've staked a claim on almost everything else." He glared at a branch of Starbucks across the street, its very existence a mute affront to everything he held sacred.

"What *is* a 'tartare' these days?" he went on. "I've seen

so-called 'tartares' of tuna, salmon, even tomato. A Japanese restaurant in New York serves what they call a 'tartare' of soybean pods, herbs, and lemon juice." He did that French thing of puffing through pursed lips. "It sounds like something women put on their face to iron out wrinkles."

In this frame of mind, we arrived at the intersection. Across Boulevard Raspail was the Rotonde and on the other side of Boulevard du Montparnasse the Café du Dôme, while, on a garden island in the middle of Raspail, Auguste Rodin's magisterial statue of Honoré de Balzac, author and gourmet, maintained its lofty disregard.

"Well, where's this tartare?" Boris asked. So we turned our backs on high culture and, as Balzac, Rodin, and Brillat-Savarin would have wished, went inside to eat.

TARTARE FOR TWO

CHARIVARI, CORNER OF RUE BRÉA AND BOULEVARD DU MONTPARNASSE

By comparison with the Dôme and Rotonde, the Charivari has a homey domesticity. On days when I'm taking people on a walk around Montparnasse, I often wait for them in the glassed-front terrace, enjoying a *café crème* and a croissant.

As a morning regular, my arrival for dinner earned a double take from the owner.

"Too early for breakfast?" I asked.

"Might be a croissant left," he said. "Go on through."

Leaving behind the crowd on the terrace, chattering and wreathed in cigarette smoke, we entered the restaurant area—and stepped back a century or more. The floor paved in tiny tiles, the varnished tables for two, the *tarif de consommation* next to the door, explaining the different prices of items at the bar and at a table; one felt what loners of earlier generations valued about such places: a sense of shared values, of complicity.

Through the window, I saw Balzac. As traffic

streamed past on both sides, he stood aloof, his mind occupied with ... what? The seething complexity of *la comédie humaine*? Or the *Rôti de bœuf à la poêle Matignon* he was no longer able to enjoy? To the French, they are the same.

The tartare, when it arrived, was of a piece with the café. The meat, sliced into tiny cubes, came in individual bowls, with boiled baby potatoes on the side, and a salad of *mesclun*, a mixture of young leaves of *mâche*, beetroot, spinach, and *roquette*. Each serving was accompanied by a dish of spicy dressing involving mustard, probably horseradish, maybe a little vinegar, which we dribbled into the chopped beef, adjusting the seasoning to our taste.

As always, Boris ate only a few mouthfuls, earning an accusingly look from the waiter as he cleared the table. For a palate as educated as his, that was more than enough. I'd seen him reject a dish after simply leaning over the plate and sniffing.

"So ... what do you think?" I asked as we drank the last of the Languedoc red and waited for coffee.

He nodded slowly, mentally weighing his reply. "I'd need to sample the other four before I made a comparison," he said finally, "and maybe try this place on another night, just to see if they're consistent."

"But . . . fifth-best in Paris?"

"Maybe. Certainly superior."

For someone who could turn up his nose at the six dishes of the €500 tasting menu at a restaurant with three Michelin stars, and ask for the cheese cart, "superior" counted as praise.

"However," he went on, "one thing did really impress me."

Boris *impressed*? I looked toward the ceiling, waiting for the thunderclap.

"What? The *frites*? The sauce?"

"No. The olives."

Olives? What olives? "You mean that little tin cup that came with our wine?"

"Yes." He leaned forward, as if not to let this valuable information travel even as far as the next table. "Normally they just empty them straight out of the can. But these had been soaked to remove the salt, then marinated in something I couldn't quite identify. Lemon juice? Or possibly grapefruit? And the texture . . . that slight crunchiness. Minced onion perhaps? A little chili . . . ?"

It was a warm night, so we walked home. By the railings of the Luxembourg Gardens, in the steps of Scott Fitzgerald and Gertrude Stein, we strolled until midnight, talking of life, literature, and condiments.

Charivari and statue of Balzac.

18

MARTHE RICHARD

SPYING FRENCH-STYLE

So far she's told us nothing, and half of that is lies.
ROBERT B. PARKER

FROM ALVIN YORK TO LAWRENCE OF ARABIA, EDDIE Rickenbacker to Edith Cavell, World War I produced numerous patriots whose feats were exaggerated in the interests of propaganda. On the French side, one of the least likely was the prostitute, swindler, Nazi collaborator, and secret agent who called herself Marthe Richard.

Born near Nancy in 1889, Marthe Betenfeld abandoned the tedium of life as a seamstress for one of prostitution. At fifteen, she was turning tricks in the local military barracks, an existence she escaped by convincing her pimp she had syphilis: the first of many lies that littered her career.

Moving to Paris, she married Henry Richer, who was something big in the Les Halles produce market. When he bought an airplane in 1912, Marthe learned to fly, and quickly set a number of records, including one for the nonstop flight from the Channel coast to Switzerland. Crowds who feted her as she landed at Zurich had no idea she only flew the start and finish, both she and the plane making the rest of the journey by train.

When her husband died in 1916, Marthe offered her services to Captain Georges Ladoux, head of the Deuxième Bureau, France's secret service. An unlikely patriot, she was probably driven by something other than love of country. Ladoux's agents included Dutch-born Margaretha Zelle, who gleaned intelligence from officers who came to see her perform seminaked "temple dances" as "Mata Hari." Zelle received a rumored FF1 million for her work, and Richer, one assumes, the same.

Ladoux dispatched Richer to Spain with orders to snare Baron Hans von Krohn, naval attaché at the German Embassy in Madrid. Since a fellow officer described the baron as *"un sadique détraqué"* (a sadistic pervert), she was well chosen for the job. The baron soon spilled every secret to her, from the names of his Spanish informants to a recipe for invisible ink.

The war over, Ladoux, unmasked as a double agent who betrayed numerous French spies to the firing squad, including Mata Hari, was found not guilty in a cover-up to preserve national face. As part of the whitewash, he wrote a book about his spymaster days. It concentrated on one of his rare successes, Marthe Richer, though the fact that *Marthe Richard, espionne au service de la France* even misspelled her name makes one skeptical about the contents. Richer responded to the book with typical self-interest. Instead of exposing Ladoux as a fraud, she demanded half his royalties, then officially changed her name to "Richard" and wrote her own memoir, even more fanciful than Ladoux's.

In *My Life as a Spy in the Service of France*, Richard paints herself as a patriot roused to vengeance by entirely imaginary German atrocities against her family. According to her, Baron von Krohn even recruited her as his agent and sent her to Argentina carrying a jar of diseased weevils with orders to infest ships carrying grain to Britain. (She lost her nerve and flushed them down the sink.) In the 1937 film of the book, Erich von Stroheim plays the von Krohn character, Baron von Ludow, as a monocled eccentric who so misses his beloved cavalry that he keeps a riding crop by his bed and, rather than sitting in a chair behind his desk, straddles a saddle.

Edwige Feuillière as spy Marthe Richard and Erich von Stroheim as her victim in Marthe Richard au service de la France.

Reborn yet again as a national heroine, Richard, fast becoming a turncoat of genius, was appointed to the Légion d'Honneur by Édouard Herriot, prime minister at the time and, conveniently, her lover. During World War II, she socialized with the collaborationist government in Vichy. When the Germans turned Paris's best brothels, including Le Chabanais and Le Sphinx, into private clubs, she catered parties there at which such stars as Édith Piaf sang for Nazi generals and their collaborators. After liberation, her underworld knowledge proved useful in smuggling some of her former clients out of the country—at a price.

Fooled by her invented past, or perhaps indifferent to it, Paris's fourth arrondissement ran her as a candidate for its municipal council. Her election didn't come a moment too soon. About to be charged with accepting FF300,000 to spring a notorious *collabo* from prison, she distracted her accusers by proposing that, to provide much-needed housing for young families, the district should convert its brothels into apartments.

The Napoleonic Code legalized prostitution but banned *proxénétisme*—pimping. Men could own brothels—Marcel Proust had an interest in two—but must employ a woman as madam and submit the women to a monthly medical examination. Just as British gentlemen went to their club to relax or talk business, those in France often met at a *bor-*

del. These were the geisha houses of France. In a relaxed setting, tended by ladies skilled in helping men relax, they could negotiate in comfort. Brothels were so important to diplomacy that the government automatically treated foreign dignitaries to a night at Le Chabanais, an excursion traditionally disguised on their itinerary as "Visit with the President of the Senate."

At any other time, legislators would have axed Richard's scheme as frivolous and impractical, but national embarrassment about the occupation inclined voters toward virtue. And, after all, *they* didn't use brothels, so what did they lose by voting to close them down? Besides, who would begrudge a newlywed couple their first home? Not only did the fourth arrondissement shut down its own *maisons de tolerance* but Richard's election also sparked a national campaign that led in 1946 to the closing of all of Paris's 180 *bordels* and 1,400 more across France. As one anguished hedonist wailed, "An era has come to an end."

A public relations triumph, the move was in other respects disastrous. Hardly any young couples wanted to begin married life in a former whorehouse, so most buildings reverted to their former use and became *hôtels de passe*, renting rooms by the hour to prostitutes who, forced back onto the streets, were no longer subject to the monthly health check, which increased the incidence of sexually transmitted diseases.

Unrepentant, Richard lived to ninety-three, pontificating to the end on the decline in morality. Asked to what she attributed her long life, she replied, straight-faced, "Abstinence."

LE SPHINX

31 BOULEVARD EDGAR-QUINET
(NOW DEMOLISHED)

April 14, 1931, was a gala night for Montparnasse. As luxury automobiles drew up just opposite the cemetery, flashbulbs exploded, illuminating the celebrities arriving to welcome Paris's latest temple of pleasure. From behind barriers, locals watched as Paris's notoriously corrupt prefect of police, Jean Chiappe, and numerous politicians, show people, and socialites, including the mayor of Montparnasse and his wife, crossed the red carpet laid over the sidewalk and entered 31 Boulevard Edgar-Quinet, passing between gilded effigies of the mythological creature from which the establishment took its name, Le Sphinx.

Until it closed in 1946, Le Sphinx would continue to attract the cream of society and show business. Colette, Hemingway, Jean-Paul Sartre and Simone de Beauvoir, and the poet Jacques Prévert all satisfied their curiosity about this new feature of Montparnasse nightlife. For Man Ray, Kisling, Foujita, Pascin, and particularly Kees van Dongen, who painted its murals, it was just another stop on their weekly beat around the quarter. It was also a must-see for foreign celebrities like Gary Cooper and Humphrey Bogart. Errol Flynn sampled its pleasures, and Marlene Dietrich used it as a cover for lesbian assignations with her lover Madeleine Sologne. A telephone line was reserved for journalists reporting on the clientele. Who would have thought that so many famous names would unashamedly patronize a brothel?

Traditionally, customers at a *bordel* paid with tokens sold by the management, which the girls traded for cash, at a profit to the house. The system faltered when Americans discovered Paris, and hankered to peer past the curtains of these infamous establishments. Guidebooks encouraged them. "The 'ladies' see no harm in you coming merely to inspect them," said one. "They will parade before you in frankest nudity, and dance with one another in a mirror-walled room, so that of their charms you may miss nothing." While this might apply to less fastidious places, so long as the visitors drank lots of overpriced champagne, a visit to the best houses required an introduction.

The proprietors of the Sphinx, Sicilian gangsters

François Spirito and Paul Carbone, already notorious in Marseilles, were the first to see that, just as a need for stateside-style entertainment inspired the creation of La Coupole, the tourists' curiosity about the demimonde could be answered by a whorehouse that doubled as a nightclub.

The moral climate of 1931 was more than receptive. Prostitution was a common inspiration for artists, including some who attended the Sphinx's opening night. In his novel *Belle de jour*, one of them, Joseph Kessel, described a young bourgeoise who moonlights as a prostitute, while another, crime writer Georges Simenon, bragged of a busy sex life during which he enjoyed the attention of ten thousand women, mostly whores.

The Sphinx, which opened at 3 p.m. and closed at dawn, advertised itself as a *bar américaine*, and copied American nightclubs in charging thirty francs—about seven dollars—to enter: the same as large dance halls of the time, such as the Coliseum. Once inside, visitors found themselves in a spacious art deco nightclub. A band played for dancing and a bar served cocktails. It might have been the first-class lounge of a transatlantic liner, said one admiring client, except for the attractive women who wandered among the tables, naked except for high-heeled shoes.

From time to time, a number of these ladies, in a version of the classic brothel "parade," appeared on a stage at one end of the salon and went through a few languid evolutions. A payment to one of the five female "supervisors" bought an hour with the woman of one's choice in a mirrored bedroom upstairs. When bandleader Duke Ellington visited, friends urged him to choose from the line of lovelies onstage. "OK," he said, "I'll take the three on the end."

Less respectable patrons of the Sphinx included swindler Alexandre Stavisky, whose fraud, involving the chain of state pawnshops known as Monts de Piété, would bring down the government in 1934. A familiar figure around Montparnasse with his mistress, Chanel model Arlette Simon, and bodyguard, "JoJo le Terreur," he was friendly with Carbone and Spirito, as well as their partner Charles Martel and Martel's wife Marguerite, known as "Martoune," who managed the Sphinx's sixty-five women, officially listed as *pensionnaires*—trainees.

Le Sphinx suffered the same fate as all French brothels in 1946. The proprietors got some satisfaction from selling its furniture and fittings at auction. "Lot No. 177," announced the auctioneer, "is the bed on which our present Minister of the Interior enjoyed so many happy hours...." (Nostalgia for those days of cultivated vice remains as strong as ever. A single ashtray from Le Sphinx recently sold at auction for €600.)

Girls at Le Sphinx.

✳ · 19 · ✳

LE SÉLECT

A HORIZONTAL TOWER OF BABEL

He was a legend in his own lunchtime.
MICHAEL FRAYN

Just after I arrived in Paris, a waiter at the Cafe Sélect, young enough to be my nephew, addressed me genially as *"jeune homme."* On my next visit, a different man took the opportunity to correct my grammar—*"une table, m'sieur"*—as he waved me to a place on the *terrasse.* By then, I had begun to recognize these Parisian habits as particularly characteristic of a café which, while respecting common politeness, thought it a duty to set outsiders straight.

The Sélect may be among the youngest of the quarter's cafés but it has the air of an earlier and more casual time.

A journalist noted approvingly its "mirrored walls, and art deco lamps, grumpy waiters, and a cat asleep on the bar." Beyond the vernal green and cream decor of the terrace, the interior of varnished tables, bentwood chairs, and leatherette banquettes drowses in a companionable gloom reminiscent of some Gauloises-permeated Café des Sports in the depths of the *vingtième*.

If its smart-mouthed staff appear out of step with the tourist-friendly style of most Montparnasse cafés, blame a history more colorful than any of its competitors. Back when the rights of waiters to a home life were less respected, the authorities allowed one establishment in each district to operate around the clock as an amenity to locals who worked unsocial hours. In Montparnasse it was the Sélect, which stayed open ostensibly for the benefit of journalists who, having put the paper to bed at 4 a.m., wanted a late supper or early breakfast.

Perhaps there were a few journalists among the clientele, but mostly it accommodated the lost, strayed, and stolen of the quarter. "At its best about 5 a.m.," said a guide of 1927. "The haven of tired 'streetwalkers' and American gluttons for *more*. Gentlemen with long wavy hair and long painted fingernails and other gentleman who, when they walk, walk 'falsetto,' toss their hips and lift their brows. But interesting." By 1936, the mix had changed only marginally. Simone de

Beauvoir noted "crop-haired lesbians who wore ties and even monocles on occasion." She and Jean-Paul Sartre, both living in the quarter at that time, though not together, dismissed such behavior as "exhibitionism" and "affected," hardly fair to the ladies who stopped by for a cognac after a long night at Le Monocle on Boulevard Edgar-Quinet, the premier club for cross-dressing females, where male evening dress and eyewear were the price of admission.

The Sélect accommodated the sapphic community, just as it did the *putes* who paused there to rest their feet after pounding the pavements, and the *petits messieurs* for whom it was a late-night haven. Better them, reasoned the management, than such Americans as the poet Hart Crane.

Crane, however gifted, was a belligerent drunk, inclined to contest a bar bill with his fists. In June 1929, his friend and publisher Harry Crosby noted in his journal, "Hart C. back from Marseilles where he slept with his thirty sailors and began again to drink Cutty Sark." Shortly after, Crane took on a load at the Sélect, punched out its waiters and the gendarmes who tried to calm him, was fined FF800 and, when he couldn't or wouldn't pay, confined in the Santé Prison. After six days, Crosby bailed him out and shipped him back to the USA to dry out. He never returned.

Writers rather than painters would always receive the most cordial welcome at the Sélect. Picasso spent time

Cross-dressing "art students," 1908.

there, but preferred the deep pockets and Hispanic culture of the Rotonde. Notoriously slow, he reached for a check only to turn it over and dash off a quick sketch in lieu of payment. On one occasion, entertaining friends at a seafood restaurant, he laid on the back of the menus the skeleton of the sole he'd just eaten, traced around it a few times with a pencil, signed the drawing, and left with the management's deepest gratitude.

In the 1950s, Le Sélect was the haunt of those American servicemen who remained in France after the war to study under the GI Bill. Had the Gene Kelly character in *An American in Paris* existed, he would have been a regular.

African-American novelist James Baldwin passed some white nights in its secluded inner corners where, sustained by cigarettes and black coffee, he wrote most of his first novel, *Giovanni's Room*. When I was researching my biography of filmmaker Luis Buñuel, who once lived around the corner of Boulevard Raspail, I used, in belated tribute, to meet there with his son Juan-Luis. No barman, Buñuel told me, was more expert in making his father's preferred tipple, a potent variation on the Negroni he called the Buñueloni.*

"Unlike some of its larger neighbours," writes Christine Graf in *The Cafés of Paris*, "Le Sélect retains its historic appeal. This is a café which still has life to it." It's true that, on its terrace, one can continue to feel, as Sisley Huddleston wrote in the 1920s, that one is at "the crossways of the world," the privileged citizen of "a horizontal Tower of Babel where there is no language that is not spoken: that stretch of sidewalk between the Gare Montparnasse and the Boulevard Saint-Michel around which live and move, and have their sometimes riotous being, representatives of every country, and members of every school of artistic expression."

---

*   Buñueloni
      1.5 measures gin
      1 measure Carpano Antica Formula vermouth
      1 measure Cinzano Rosso sweet vermouth
      Stir and pour over ice in a highball glass. Garnish with an orange slice.

TERRANCE ON THE *TERRASSE*

"Would you describe yourself as displaying 'a riotous being?'" I asked Terrance Gelenter.

"I have my moments," he said. "But listen. I read your last book. You didn't libel me even once. What, I'm boring you?"

We were sitting on the terrace of the Sélect. It was Sunday morning, the time Terrance—pronounced, he insists, in the French fashion, "Terr-*onse*"—describes on his website as "office hours," those moments in his often frenzied progress around the city when he pauses to receive visitors, sell them one of his self-published books, and, unless they are very quick on their feet, serenade them with a wobbly "I Left My Heart in San Francisco."

True boulevardiers, survivors in the tradition of Harold Stearns and those eccentrics who loitered at the Dingo and Falstaff, are thin on the ground in today's Paris, but Terrance is as authentic an example as you will find, one of those individuals who, lacking a creative gift, found a role living in the shadows of art. Squint your eyes even a little and you could imagine him as the barker outside some Pigalle club, hissing to passing sailors, "They're naked—and they *dance!*" or perhaps a *bouquiniste*, proprietor of a green-painted stall along the Seine, responding with a wink to the nervous tourist who inquires, "*Quelque'chose neuf de Olympia?*"

He might even be, conceivably, the reincarnation of Frank Harris, journalist, editor, friend of George Bernard Shaw and Oscar Wilde, and lover, he boasted, of more than two thousand women, details of whom he claimed to have card-indexed.

Only five feet six inches tall, sharply dressed, with a mass of slicked-back hair and a bushy waxed mustache, tweaked at the ends and, like the hair, suspiciously black, Harris resembled a bantam rooster with the barnyard's loudest crow. John Dos Passos reviled him as "an objectionable little man. He was sallow as a gypsy. He had bat ears, dark hair with a crinkle in it that grew low on the forehead, and a truculent moustache. People remarked on the richness of his bass voice. His charm was great, particularly for the opposite sex. He had the gift of the gab to a sublime degree and a streak of deep scoundrelism that was the ruin of him." But such gibes rolled off Harris like water off that glistening hairdo. In a long and eventful life, he'd been reamed by experts.

Harris spent his declining years on the Côte d'Azur, composing a fanciful autobiography that described a mere few hundred of his conquests. When every reputable publisher rejected *My Life and Loves*, Harris offered the manuscript to Sylvia Beach, who had, after all, published *Ulysses*. Accepting her refusal with a shrug, he looked around the shelves of Shakespeare and Company and asked, "What would you recommend to read on the train back to Nice?"

Deadpan, Beach asked, "Do you know *Little Women*?"

Harris's eyes lit up. "No!" he said. "But it sounds *very* interesting." What he made of Louisa May Alcott's staid tale of four sisters growing up in rural America, we will never know.

Often crass, Harris could also be kind. Following his trial and imprisonment, Oscar Wilde had few friends, among whom Harris was the most effective. He paid his debts and spirited him to the Mediterranean, urging him to lie low until the hunt died down. Vain hope. "Even in La Napoule there is romance," Wilde wrote dreamily. "It takes the form of fisher-lads, who draw great nets, and are strangely perfect. I was in Nice recently. Romance there is a profession, plied beneath the moon." Before he died, Wilde dedicated his play *An Ideal Husband* to Harris, "a slight tribute to his power and distinction as an artist, his chivalry and nobility as a friend."

"Gotta go," Terrance said suddenly, bolting up from the table. Down the terrace, half a dozen tourists were peering around nervously. Corralling them like errant sheep, he shepherded them to a larger table at the other end. As I stood up, a cough from our waiter drew my attention to the bill. It seemed I was paying not only for our coffees but for the croissant and *cafe crème* consumed by Terrance before I arrived. Reaching for my wallet, I consoled myself that I was reaffirming a venerable tradition.

Ça va, Pablo?

✳ ·20· ✳

CIMETIÈRE DU MONTPARNASSE

*His soul had approached that region where dwell the
vast hosts of the dead. He was conscious of, but could
not apprehend, their wayward and flickering existence.
His own identity was fading out into a grey impalpable
world: the solid world itself, which these dead had one
time reared and lived in, was dissolving and dwindling.*

JAMES JOYCE, "THE DEAD"

BEFORE THE CITY OF PARIS ABSORBED MONTPARNASSE IN
1669, the portion of the hilltop occupied by today's cemetery was its potter's field. The name goes back to the Old
Testament. After betraying Christ, Judas returned the
thirty pieces of silver paid by the priests of the Temple, then
hanged himself. Since a suicide couldn't be buried in con-
secrated ground, nor could the silver, now tainted as "blood

money," be returned to the coffers, the priests resolved both problems with a creative compromise. Buying an infertile field where potters dug clay, they interred Judas there, and thereafter reserved it as a place "to bury strangers in." Over centuries, "potter's field" came to mean any graveyard for the anonymous dead.

By the time Georges-Eugène Haussmann rebuilt Paris, the Cimetière du Montparnasse had become, as it remains, one of its more discreet resting places. The jumbled stonescapes of Père Lachaise and Montmartre have their admirers, but, for me, among Paris graveyards, it alone possesses true gravity and calm. Visiting, I'm reminded of those walled cemeteries outside villages in Normandy or Charente, gated communities of the departed where generations rest in neighborly comfort: "robed in the long friends," as Dylan Thomas wrote, "the grains beyond age."

It is also, traditionally, the appropriate place to commemorate the achievements of a lifetime that don't necessarily merit a statue in some public park. Just as artists rejected by the annual Salon held their own Salon des Refusés, it celebrates those people who, for good or ill, did things Their Way.

One such person was Charles Pigeon (1838–1915). Believing the invention of a gasoline lamp entitled him to special treatment even in death, Pigeon topped his spacious monument with a life-size bronze effigy of his wife and himself reclining in a double bed, he in frock coat, cravat, and, alert for inspiration even in death, with pen and note-book in hand.

An even stranger cenotaph honors the poet Charles Baudelaire. Financed by a committee of artists disgusted that his actual grave, elsewhere in the cemetery, post-humously adopted him into the family of a stepfather he despised, the project had enemies from the start. For ten

Tomb of Charles Pigeon.

years, sponsors wrangled over the morality of erecting a monument to the "decadent" author of *Les fleurs du mal* (Flowers of Evil) and in particular *Les paradis artificiels* (Artificial Paradises), which celebrated the pleasures of opium and hashish.

Auguste Rodin, first choice to create the monument, lost patience, and surrendered the commission to José de Charmoy, a young unknown who worked the controversy into his design. Baudelaire appears as an almost anonymous corpse, supine and wrapped in a shroud. Above him, a figure who might be the Angel of Death, but whom others have called a "satanic dreamer," broods on a fate appropriate to someone of Baudelaire's radical tendencies. An inscription addresses Death as "old Captain" and urges him to "plunge us into the abyss. Hell or Heaven, what does it matter? At the limits of the unknown, we find the new."

More recent arrivals in the cemetery reflect an equally indeterminate view of the afterlife. Jean-Paul Sartre and his companion Simone de Beauvoir share, despite Beauvoir's feminist convictions, a common grave. Samuel Beckett, most reticent of playwrights, rests under a simple black slab. On the equally modest grave of actor Philippe Noiret, a marble cat curls in perpetual tranquility, in contrast to the bulbous, grinning feline, covered in fractured tile, that

Monument to Charles Baudelaire, Montparnasse Cemetery.

sculptor Niki de Saint Phalle created for the tomb of her assistant Ricardo Menon.

Fans have so piled the tomb of singer Serge Gainsbourg with potted plants, photographs, and flowers that one might easily overlook the slabs of white stone, barely knee-high, that mark the graves of Man Ray and his wife Juliet. Hers, decorated with an undistinguished photograph of the couple, is inscribed "JULIET MAN RAY 1911–1991. TOGETHER AGAIN." His monument, as if to remonstrate with those intent on advertising their importance, bears, almost invisibly, the enigmatic epitaph he wrote himself: "UNCONCERNED BUT NOT INDIFFERENT."

Appropriate to its position astride the fence between death and the afterlife, Montparnasse Cemetery, while well furnished with angels, boasts, for a supposedly Catholic country, surprisingly few images of Jesus or the Virgin. Rather, the tone is ecumenical, veering to the secular, with a strong Judaic admixture. Some visitors even to gentile tombs follow the Jewish custom of placing a pebble on the grave. Others, perceiving the cemetery, like Montparnasse itself, as a place of transition, of arrival and departure, introduce a Parisian variation and leave a Metro ticket instead.

DESPERATELY SEEKING SUSAN

"I thought I'd come over and visit Susan Sontag," said Kevin Jackson, calling from deepest Cambridgeshire. I could almost hear the crack of willow on leather from the cricket pitch next door to his cottage, and smell the port and Stilton cheese.

Kevin was one of my oldest English friends. Author of books on the literature of money, the voyage of the *Mayflower*, and a history of the British belief in ghosts, he also holds the rank of regent in the College of Pataphysics, that association of literary eccentrics formed in memory of Alfred Jarry, author of *Ubu Roi* and *The Passion Considered as an Uphill Bicycle Race*.

Visits from Kevin, though always a pleasure, often veer in unexpected directions. A few years ago, we'd shared a midnight walk in the steps of Philippe Soupault's Surrealist novel *Last Nights of Paris*, a stroll that spiraled into realms of the hallucinatory and, arguably, supernatural. Even for him, however, a call on Susan Sontag, eminent American essayist and author of *Against Interpretation* and *Notes on Camp*, promised to be stranger.

"Isn't she ... um, *dead*?"

"Indeed. Since 2004."

A pattern was emerging. "But she's buried ...?"

"... in Paris ..."

"... and in Cimetière du Montparnasse?"

"Precisely."

On a cold, wet, gray Tuesday a few weeks later, we strolled up Boulevard Edgar-Quinet and turned into Paris's most tranquil graveyard. Over six feet tall, wearing a long black overcoat and leaning on a cane to favor an injured foot, Kevin radiated gravitas. The few people we passed lowered their eyes in deference. A general? Perhaps a head of state on an incognito visit? Not that I would be so crass as to blow his cover, least of all in a place that invited, even demanded one accept people at their own valuation. *"De mortuis nil nisi bonum"* counsels one of etiquette's oldest rules—Of the dead, say nothing but good.

At a pace dictated by Kevin's injury—but who hurries in a graveyard?—we navigated the central avenue, lined with wet and leafless chestnut trees. At the first intersection, we paused to consult the guide acquired at the guardians' lodge. The names of those buried here was a roll call of the great: Baudelaire, Beckett, Beauvoir, Duras, Man Ray, Maupassant, Soutine, and ... ah yes: Sontag.

Reoriented, we headed deeper into the forest of marble and stone.

"Did you know her well?" I asked.

"Susan? We usually got together anytime she was in England. And I visited her a few times in New York."

"So what did you do together?"

"Oh, you know. Walked. Chatted."

I tried to imagine bantering with the author of *Illness as Metaphor*. Such encounters with the admired great can go badly wrong, particularly if the host has a malicious sense of humor. When the young Curtis Harrington, later an eminent filmmaker, called on James Whale, director of *Frankenstein*, Whale, both gay and a wit, suggested, "Just to make it interesting for me, let's do this. For each question I answer, you remove a piece of clothing."

Another technique was developed by Hemingway's friend Bill Ryall, who wrote as William Bolitho. To any admirer arriving uninvited at his home in the south of France, he proposed, "You will talk for an hour and I will talk for an hour." Few survived this trial by conversation, for reasons explained by James Thurber. "If I were the man told off to speak last, I would not be able to take in what the other man was saying because I would be trying to think of something to say when my turn came. This would lead to the stiff posture, the horrible smile, the inattentive monosyllabic interjection, and the glazed expression of the eye. When my host's hour was up, I am afraid I would only be able to repeat, over and over, 'This is a mighty nice place you've got here.'"

I could see myself becoming just as tongue-tied in Sontag's presence. "Do you remember any topics of these chats?" I asked, hoping to benefit from Kevin's experience the next time I encountered a legend.

"Different things." He stopped to remember. "She loved *The Goon Show*. She and her son David could do all the characters."

The silly voices of Hercules Grytpype-Thynne and Dan "The Famous" Eccles, alter egos of Peter Sellers and Spike Milligan, mimicked by the author of *Styles of Radical Will*? Would it have helped in interviewing Alain Robbe-Grillet if I had done my Bluebottle imitation? Before I could play out such an incongruity, another intersection sent us back to our map.

As we puzzled over it, Kevin said, "I was surprised at how much she liked Shakespeare. I think it was on our first meeting in New York. She said, "When people ask me who my favorite writer is, I say 'Shakespeare.' This tends to surprise them, because they expect me to say 'Mallarmé' or 'Artaud' or 'Nietzsche' or 'Kafka' or 'Celan' or 'Camus,' because those are the people I write about. But I wrote about them because they needed to be better known. Everyone knows about Shakespeare, and he deserves that. He is incomparable."

Our new direction sent us into an area where only narrow paths, hardly more than sheep tracks, ran between the tightly packed graves. Every few meters, a familiar name caught our eye. Being almost the only visitors conferred an air of privacy. We might have been visiting friends.

"Here we are," Kevin called from the next alley.

I found him contemplating a horizontal slab of wet black marble. It bore no message beyond Sontag's name and the years of her birth and death.

"Was she religious?"

"Not as far as I knew. It's certainly not in her work."

So why did she ask to be buried here? Perhaps because it was an island of calm in the torrent of time that poured past beyond the walls. Somewhere to be quiet, "robed with the long friends, the grains beyond age."

But the lack of an epitaph clashed with my perception of a woman who always had something to say; the kind who would arrive halfway through a dinner party and demand, "Well, what's the conversation?"

"So what's she doing buried in France?"

"One of her earliest ambitions had been to study medicine and become a doctor," Kevin said. "This had been, literally, a lifesaver, since, when she was first diagnosed with cancer, she hurled herself into an intensive period of research, and discovered that France offered a much more aggressive treatment than any permitted in the USA. She came here and was duly cured, though not permanently, alas.

"Her beauty was fading in the years I knew her," he went on as we walked back to the gate, "not helped by a massive car crash, more cancer, more chemotherapy—and she put on a lot of weight in her last years. Yet there was something still very attractive about her, and though she was probably more gay than straight, she did not 'read' as sapphic at all. Though she was formidable, she could exercise a traditional feminine charm when she felt so inclined."

He stopped. "She was vain—but she had a great deal of justification."

Said with such respect, it sounded like an epitaph. Just not sufficiently so. To summarize a life in a few lines needed a touch of the poet: in her case, of Shakespeare.

Memory pulled me back to another sad wet day, but in London, and a memorial service at St. Paul's, the actors' church in Covent Garden. Coming in late, I stood at the back. A rambling reminiscence from an old friend gave plenty of time to browse the plaques mounted on the back wall that commemorated other famous theatrical departed. The nearest was for actress Vivien Leigh—just her name, dates of birth and death, and two lines from *Antony and Cleopatra*—the words Cleopatra's maid Charmian speaks over her dead mistress.

Now boast thee, death, in thy possession lies
A lass unparallel'd.

I didn't think Vivien wouldn't mind sharing—nor Shakespeare, come to that. His work was rich enough in great lines to commemorate a regiment; indeed an army.

Had this been a film, a gust of wind would have stirred the dead leaves and a spectral voice intoned the words. But this was Paris, city of the secular and rational. So instead, an ambulance raced by, siren whooping, en route to the Hôpital Val-de-Grâce, and we went for coffee at La Coupole.

THE BEST NIGHTCLUB THAT EVER WAS .

Call to me all my sad captains. Let's
have one other gaudy night.
WILLIAM SHAKESPEARE,
ANTONY AND CLEOPATRA

Samuel Putnam, not for nothing a translator of that meditation on human folly, *Don Quixote*, contributed a glum epitaph for the quarter between the wars.

> *Such was the Montparnasse we knew: a weird little*
> *land crowded with artists, alcoholics, prostitutes,*
> *pimps, poseurs, college boys, tourists, society slum-*
> *mers, spendthrifts, beggars, homosexuals, drug*
> *addicts, nymphomaniacs, sadists, masochists,*
> *thieves, gamblers, confidence men, mystics, fakers,*

> *paranoiacs, political refugees, anarchists, "dukes"*
> *and "countesses," men and women without a coun-*
> *try; a land filled with a gaiety sometimes real and*
> *often feigned, filled with sorrow, suffering, poverty,*
> *frustration, bitterness, tragedy, suicide. Not only*
> *was there never any place like it; Montparnasse it-*
> *self had never been before and never will be again*
> *what it was in the 1920s. For it was essentially a*
> *part of the first* après-guerre. *And from 1929 on it*
> *began dying.*

No doubt true. But if *Don Quixote* celebrates any-thing, it is the unquenchability of romance; the exhilaration of the empty gesture; the poignancy of the dying fall—all characteristics ostentatiously on show in the great days of Montparnasse.

If I could go back to those times, to what place and time would I return? To eavesdrop on the gossip at the Dôme? Sit in the Rotonde and pay Modigliani a franc to sketch me? Watch the *poules de luxe* stroll around the salon of Le Sphinx? Get my clock cleaned sparring with Hemingway in his apartment on rue Férou?

Well, in my case, none of those—because they are so fully documented that to visit them would be like taking one of those tours where a bus retraces the same route every hour to a taped commentary that, with each circuit, slips a little further out of sync with what's outside the window.

Instead, imagine it's 1929 and follow me down rue Campagne-Première, past Man Ray's old studio and the Hôtel Istria where the more prosperous Montparnos enjoyed their *cinq à septs*, past the home of painters Per Krohg and Othon Friesz, and of Kiki's friend Thérèse Maure, renamed by Robert Desnos "Thérèse Treize," i.e., "Thérèse Thirteen." Past No. 17, where resided Mina Loy, author of "Lunar Baedecker," and Rainer Maria Rilke when he was secretary to Auguste Rodin; all the way down to the intersection with Boulevard du Montparnasse, where once stood Le Jockey, called by Hemingway "the best nightclub that ever was."

It's long gone, of course, replaced by a bland modern building. But it survives in stories—of Hemingway dancing with Josephine Baker, who, before stepping out into the night, opened her long fur coat to show him she was naked under it. Or the proprietor, American artist Hilaire Hiler, interrupting a client about to take his life in the restroom and persuading him to kill himself instead at the Dôme and so ruin business for his competitor. Stories some of which— who knows?—may even be true.

The life of Le Jockey was that of a mayfly. The onetime sculptor's studio was the Auberge des Rouliers until 1921 and Le Caméléon until 1923, after which it was Le Jockey until it closed in 1930. Hiler, born Hiler Harzberg, opened it when he was just twenty-five and newly arrived in Paris. A former jockey named Miller sold him a share of the business to settle some gambling debts.

The name was a swipe at that bastion of Parisian privilege, the Jockey Club de Paris, which inhabited palatial premises on rue Scribe, within sight of the Opéra. There any resemblance ended. In an attempt to imitate a western saloon, Hiler decorated the exterior with stylized images of cowboys and Indians. The interior, according to a 1927 guide, offered "low, cracked ceilings, tattered walls covered with posters, cartoons painted with shoe polish and a sign reading 'The only client we ever lost, died.'" Hiler's own sketches show the report erred, if anything, on the sunny side: a bare wooden bar with shelves of bottles behind, a few tables around the walls, and a crowd of what look like shabby barflies but were actually Robert Desnos, Jules Pascin, and the cream of the quarter's eccentrics.

According to Robert McAlmon, "almost anybody of the writing, painting, musical, gigoloing, whoring, pimping, or drinking world was apt to turn up at the Jockey." The club soon became notorious as an *'after'*—somewhere to party on once the Dôme and Coupole closed. "Go at 11 o'clock," advised a guidebook. "See famous painters and

The Jockey, with Hilaire Hiler's decorations.

the real Bon Vivants of Paris. An indescribable atmosphere."
After midnight, the place roared. "People were drinking,
singing, talking, laughing, in a cloud of smoke from all the
tobacco in the world," wrote artist Jean Oberlé. "From time
to time, we went out on the boulevard to take a good breath
of fresh air, and then plunged in again."

There was a half-hearted pretense at supplying food.
Oberlé remembers "a small staircase leading to the kitchen,
where a Chilean chef was officiating. The laughing face of
this friendly Indian sometimes appeared between the cur-

tains, wearing a chef's toque." Almost no one ate at the tiny tables. Desnos used one to compose poems, scribbling them on paper napkins, with which the lone waiter kept him supplied. Once the irrepressible Kiki inaugurated a nightly talent show with herself as mistress of ceremonies, the cook gave up, and amended the chalked list of "House Specialties" to include, after "Welsh Rarebit," "Kiki dances and sings."

"Everyone does a turn," said Kiki, describing a typical night. "A big Russian tries to do Cossack dances. Floriane dances quite lasciviously, even though she's barely five feet tall." A discovery of Louis Aragon, Floriane was by profession a Spanish dancer, with a repertoire of fandangos and a wardrobe of frilly flamenco dresses, both of which she abandoned at the Jockey. "She performed an oriental dance," wrote McAlmon, "twisting her long body without hips. Her small firm breasts oscillated back and forth as she leaned back to the ground, her arms undulating, her mouth quivering, adorable in intensity and emotion."

In her own performances, Kiki made up in energy what she lacked in talent. "I can't sing when I'm not drunk," she said, "and not when I'm doing anything else. (I'm astonished by these women can sing and pee at the same time.) My ear is good but not my memory. Fortunately my friend Treize feeds me the lines." Her bawdy songs, not to mention some revealing glimpses under her skirt, made her one of the sights of Montparnasse. Once word got around, automobiles jammed the narrow street and climbed the sidewalks. Noting the improved quality of the clientele, Treize took to circulating with a bowler hat after each turn, divvying up the contributions among the performers.

On weekends, a professional band took over, dispensing an incongruous program entirely consistent with the Jockey. According to a somewhat baffled contemporary description, "Les Cubains sing the last novelties of their native tropic isles to the tremulous notes of guitars which wail plaintively in a moment of song, only to break spontaneously into the most rollicking syncopated jazz and 'Hula Hula' tunes to disperse the pensive silence of the smoke-filled room, and half a hundred feet spring into the center of the small floor to beat in unison the rhythm the whole world responds to."

THE JOCKEY

CORNER OF RUE CAMPAGNE-PREMIÈRE AND BOULEVARD DU MONTPARNASSE

Kiki called the Jockey's community "a little family" but a better comparison would have been a village, for which the club furnished what Michel Georges-Michel called its *kermesse*: the annual fair.

In the early days, piano music was supplied by Ben, an African-American, one of many who frequented the club. Another regular was Joe Alex, the Martiniquais actor and dancer who would carry Josephine Baker onstage for her sensational premiere appearance in the *Revue nègre*. An occasional performer at the tiny movie studios in suburban Montreuil, headquarters of the predominantly Russian Albatros Films, Alex was probably responsible for director Jean Epstein re-creating the club, as "Le Jokey," in his 1924 film *Le lion des Mogols*. Kiki is visible briefly in this sequence, lost in a mob of dancers. Russian émigré Ivan Mosjoukine starred as an exiled Asian prince adrift in the fleshpots of Paris. Short, long-faced, a little ridiculous, Mosjoukine was favored at one time to replace Rudolph Valentino, but he would have been at best a small boy's idea of a Latin lover. Even so, Kiki, hungry for a screen career, added him to her lengthening list of lovers. At the end of the night, they would slip away to the Hôtel Istria, leaving Mosjoukine's sports car parked outside the Jockey, an advertisement for the club and Kiki both.

Kiki can be seen, again dancing, in another film of the same year, this time actually shot at the Jockey. Marcel L'Herbier, later a famous director, designed *La galerie des monstres* and his favorite actor Jaque Catelain directed it. What survives of this oddity are some carnival scenes, with grotesque costumes, of no more interest than scores of other experimental misfires, except that they give glimpses of three women who deserve that distinctively French designation *"monstres sacrés"*—sacred monsters: individuals whose fame elevates them to another plane of existence.

One is fifteen-year-old Lois Moran, the American actress who would bewitch Scott Fitzgerald, and inspire the character of Rosemary Hoyt in his last completed novel, *Tender Is the Night*. The second is former Ziegfeld showgirl Florence "Flossie"

Martin, who helped win the Dingo Bar its sulfurous reputation.

The third, however, is Kiki, credited, in a gesture to her then-lover, as "Kiki Ray." She dances happily, clapping, grinning, and wearing, for once, a long dress in a summery print that disguises her lack of lingerie. Perhaps Montparnasse was, as Apollinaire grumbled, "a quarter of crazies," but if they were mad, it was a fine wild madness with a touch about it of the poet. Those first drunken student explorers of this hill had been right. There were muses here.

Some Montparnos in front of The Jockey, including Kiki, Ezra Pound, Jean Cocteau, Man Ray, Bill Bird, and Hilaire Hiler.

ACKNOWLEDGMENTS

MANY THANKS TO KEVIN JACKSON, NEIL PEARSON, Terrance Gelenter, Tony Foster for his indispensable map, the staff and management of Le Charivari, Le Sélect, and La Coupole, Louise Baxter and Marie-Dominique Montel, and my editor Peter Hubbard as well as all at Harper Perennial, in particular Nick Amphlett and copy editor Amy Robbins.

INDEX

Abbey of Solesmes, 117

absinthe, 72–77

Absinthe Drinkers (Degas), 74

Académie Carmen, xiii (map),
51–53, 57

Académie Colarossi, xiii (map), 50,
51–56

Académie de la Grande-Chaumière,
51, 52–54, 60

Académie du Caméleo, 56–57

Académie du Montparnasse, 56–57

Académie Julian, 48, 50

Académie Ranson, 57

Académie Szabo, 57

Against Interpretation (Sontag), 206

Aguilard, Marie-Auguste, 162–63

Albatros Films, 221–22

alchemy, 75–77

alcohol, 104, 108
    absinthe, 72–77
    Prohibition, 25

Alcott, Louisa May, 198

Alex, Joe, 221

*À l'heure de l'Observatoire: Les
    amoureux (Observatory Time: The
    Lovers*, Ray), 99

Alice B. Toklas Cookbook, The
    (Toklas), 166

"almanacs," 96–98

ambergris, 140

American in Paris, An (film), 194–95

American League of Writers,
    130–31

Annah la Javanaïse (Gauguin), 69–71

Anti-Fascist League, 130–31

anti-Semitism, 2–3

Antony and Cleopatra (Shakespeare),
    212, 214

Apaches (street gang), 113, 134

Apollinaire, Guillaume, 2, 37–38,
    47–48, 61, 64–65, 89, 140, 223

Aragon, Louis, 95–97, 219

Archipenko, Alexander, 89

Arfvidson, André, 100

Aristophanes, 12

art schools, 47–60

At the Sign of the Black Manikin,
    xiii (map), 30, 35–36

Auberge des Rouliers, 216–17

Auberge de Venise, 125–27

Aux Îles Marquises, 64

Avenue Denfert-Rochereau, xiii (map)

Avenue du Maine, xiii (map), 16

Bachicha (Juan Bautista
    Deambroggio), 139–40

Baker, Josephine, xviii, xxii, 137,
    159, 166, 216, 221

Bal Bullier, xiii (map), 20, 78,
    79–81, 135
Bal de la Grande-Chaumière, 18–19,
    21–23
Bal de Printemps, 19–20
Bald, Wambly, 28–29, 107
Baldwin, James, 194–95
Bal Nègre, 157–60
bals jardins (dance gardens), 17–19,
    21–23, 48, 113
bals musette (dance halls), 16–23,
    132, 134–42
Balzac, Honoré de (statue), 174,
    175–76, 178
Bande à Bonnot (street gang), 113
bar américaine, 188–89
Barney, Natalie Clifford, 27
Barry, Philip, 129
Bateau Lavoir, 84
Baudelaire, Charles
    Les fleurs du mal (Flowers of
        Evil), 202–3, 204
    Little Poems in Prose, 36, 59, 73
Beach, Sylvia, 30–33, 145, 198
Beadle, Charles, 146
beauty spots, 106
Beauvoir, Simone de, 160, 186,
    192–93, 203
Beaux-Arts, École des, 48–51, 57
Bechet, Sidney, 159
Beckett, Samuel, 149–50, 203
Belle de jour (Kessel), 188
la belle époque, 22, 155
Belloc, Hilaire, 109
Betenfeld, Marthe. *See* Richard,
    Marthe
Bianco, Eduardo, 139–40

Bigot, Alexandre, 100
Bird, Bill, 31–32
Black Manikin, xiii (map), 30, 35–36
Black Sun Press, 30, 32
Blue Train, 155
boeuf tartare, 169–78
Bogart, Humphrey, 25, 30, 187
La bohème (Puccini), 84
Bois de Bologne, 117
Bolitho, William (Bill Ryall), 208–9
Boni & Liveright, 3
Bonnot Gang (street gang), 113
bordels, 29, 183–90
Boucher, Alfred, 87–89
Bouguereau, William, 85
Boulevard du Montparnasse, xiii
    (map), 79–81, 125, 175–78
Boulevard Edgar-Quinet, 157,
    186–90
Boulevard Raspail, xiii (map),
    125, 195
Bourdelle, Antoine, 54, 57
Boyle, Kay, 26, 34, 111
Bragança, Nadejda de, 146
Brâncuși, Contantin, 64–65, 89
Brasserie Lipp, 165
Breton, André, 28, 95, 96–98,
    116–18
Bridget Jones's Diary (film), 143
Brillat-Savarin, Jean Anthelme,
    165, 174
Broca, Henri, 95, 107–8
Broom (periodical), 33
brothels, 29, 183–90
Bruce, Kathleen, 55–56
Bryher (Annie Winifred Ellerman),
    27, 30–31

Bullier, François, 80–81
Buñuel, Juan Luis, 195
Buñuel, Luis, 27, 28, 135, 195
Buñueloni, 195, 195n
Burroughs, William, 149–50

Café Charivari, xiii (map), 169,
    175–78
café-concert, 19
Café du Dôme, xiii (map), xix, 4–5,
    109–10, 113–14
    closing, 217
    freeloaders, 7–8
    Ernest de Gegenbach and, 116–18
    terrace, 6–7
cafés
    as gathering places, 4
    as "home," 3–4
    social and racial tensions, 2–4
    telephones and, 4
    in "the quarter," 1
Cafés of Paris, The (Graf), 195
cakewalk (dance), 136
La Californie, xiii (map), 15–16, 73
Callaghan, Morley, 2–3, 35
Le Caméléon, 216–17
Camus, Albert, 160
cancan, 18–19, 80–81
Candide (Voltaire), 149
cannabis, 25, 159
Capa, Robert, 44
Carbone, Paul, 187–88, 189
Caron, Charlotte, 56, 64, 67, 77
Carrière, Jean-Claude, 28
Casablanca (film), 24–25, 30
Castle, Irene, 136, 139
Castle, Vernon, 136

Catacombs, xiii (map), 15
Catelain, Jacques, 222
Céline, Louis-Ferdinand, 135–36
Cendrars, Blaise, 89
Centre Sportif Universitaire Jean
    Sarrailh, 81
Cézanne, Paul, 47
Le Chabanais, 183–84
Chagall, Marc, 89
chahut (uproar), 18–19, 20
Charles II (England), 13
Charleston (dance), 137
Charmoy, José de, 203
Charters, Jimmy, 110–11, 113–14
Chemins de Fer de l'Ouest, 161–64
Chevalier, Maurice, 159
Chez Rosalie, xiii (map), 85, 86, 168
Chiappe, Jean, 186
Chicago Tribune (Paris), 28, 32–33
Chirico, Giorgio de, 157, 158
Christian Science Monitor, 28
Cimetière du Montparnasse, xiii
    (map), 44, 45, 76, 107, 200–213
cités d'artistes, xiii (map), 84–90
Cité Taberlet, xiii (map), 84–85
Civilization in the United States
    (Stearns), 29–30
Claudel, Camille, 51
"Clean, Well-Lighted Place, A"
    (Hemingway), 82
close dancing, 134–35
Closerie des Lilas, xiii (map), 8,
    72–81, 125
Cluny (Abbey Museum), 76
Coates, Robert M., 32
cocaine, 25, 108
Cocteau, Jean, 137

coffee, 16, 73
Colarossi, Filippo, 50, 51–52, 55–56, 57
Colette, 186
Colin, Paul, 159
Coliseum, 188
Coming Struggle for Power, The (Strachey), 130
Commengé, Béatrice, 147
Communism, 129–31
concierges, 42–46
Contact (periodical), 33
Contact Editions, 31, 32–33
Cooper, Gary, 187
Corelli, Marie, 62
corsets, 139
Cotton Club, 159
La Coupole, xiii (map), xvii–xxiii, 9–10, 151–53, 188
    ballroom, 138–42
    changes over time, xxii, xxiii
    closing, 217
    Kiki of Montparnasse and, 107–8
    opening in 1927, xviii–xix, 4–5
    pillar and pilaster art, xxi–xxiii
"Crack-Up, The" (Fitzgerald), 124
Crane, Hart, 9–10, 193
Crèmerie Caron, 56, 64, 77
Crèmerie Leduc, 56
crèmeries, 56, 168
Crosby, Harry, 27, 30, 193
cross-dressing, 193, 194
Crowley, Aleister, 36
Crowninsheild, Frank, 122
Cubism, 64, 136
Cunard, Nancy, 27, 30, 32
Customs House, xiii (map), 14–15

Dada movement, 28, 95
Dalí, Salvador, 27, 93
dance
    bals jardins (dance gardens), 17–19, 21–23, 48, 113
    bals musette (dance halls), 16–23, 132, 134–42
danses de société, 132–42
Darantière, Maurice, 145
"Dead, The" (Joyce), 200
Deambroggio, Juan Bautista ("Bachicha"), 139–40
Degas, Edgar, 74
Delaunay, Robert, 89
Delessert, Gabriel, 18
Delius, Frederick, 59, 68, 75, 76
Desnos, Robert, 158, 216, 217, 219
Désossé, Valentin ("Boneless Valentin"), 80–81
Deuxième Bureau, 180–81
Dial, The, 29–30
Dietrich, Marlene, 187
Dingo Bar, xiii (map), 110–11, 125, 196, 222–23
dirty books (DB). *See* erotica
Donleavy, J. P., 150
Don Quixote (Cervantes), 214–15
Doolittle, Hilda (H.D.), 31
Dos Passos, John, 3, 120, 197
douaniers (customs officers), 15, 64–65, 98
Doumer, Paul, 112–13
Dufresne, Charles, xxi–xxii
Duhamel, George, xxii–xxiii
du Maurier, George, 61–63
Durand-Ruel, Paul, 65–67
Durrell, Lawrence, 145

Eater of Darkness, The (Coates), 32

École des Beaux-Arts, 48–51, 57

Eiffel, Gustav, 87–88

Eliot, T. S., xvii

Elizabeth I (England), 33

Ellerman, Annie Winifred ("Bryher"), 27, 30–31

Ellerman, John, 30–31

Ellington, Duke, 189

Éluard, Paul, 93

Émile-Bayard, Jean, 58

Epstein, Jean, 221–22

Epstein, Julius J., 24

Epstein, Philip G., 24

Ericsson, Ida, 70, 75

Ernst, Max, 28, 85

erotica, 31, 91–101, 144–53

Erwitt, Elliot, 84

Escaped Cock, The (Lawrence), 32

Escoffier, Georges Auguste, 172

ether, 47

Europe, James Reese, 136

Exposition Universelle (1889), 84–85

Exposition Universelle (1900), 87–88

Falstaff, 107, 125, 196

Fantômas series, 113, 118

Fay, Bernard, 38

Feininger, Lyonel, 51

Fels, Florent, xxi–xxii

femmes de ménage (maids of all work), 38–46

Feuillade, Louis, 113

Feuillière, Edwige, 182

Fillard, Benoît, 21–22

Finnegan's Wake (Joyce), 30, 33

Fisher, M. F. K., 170

Fitzgerald, Zelda (wife of F. Scott), 38–39, 123–24, 126, 137

Fitzgerald, F. Scott, xx
    "The Crack-Up," 124
    family nanny, 38–39
    The Great Gatsby, 123, 125, 126
    The Last Tycoon, 119–20
    and Donald Ogden Stewart, 119–20, 123–27
    Tender is the Night, 222

Flanner, Janet (Genêt), 28–29

Les fleurs du mal (Flowers of Evil) (Baudelaire), 202–3

Floriane, 219

Flory, Régine, 116

"Flossie" (Florence Martin), 110, 222–23

Flynn, Errol, 187

Folies, Bergère, xviii, 137

food, 56, 165–78. *See also* cafés *and names of specific cafés*
    boeuf tartare, 169–78
    crèmeries, 56, 168

Ford, Charles Henri, 146

Ford, Ford Madox, 19

forehead band, 139

Foujita, Tsuguharu, 48, 49, 85, 100, 104, 107, 108, 186

Foundation for National Culture, 89

Four Horsemen of the Apocalypse (film), 138

fox-trot (dance), 137

France, Anatole, 113

Franco-Prussian War (1870-71), 27–28, 56

Frankenstein (film), 208
Frank, Robert, 84
Fraux, Ernest, xix
Frayn, Michael, 191
Friesz, Othon, 216
Frogs, The (Aristophanes), 12

Gainsbourg, Serge, 205
La galerie des monstres (film), 94, 222
Garbo, Greta, 168
Gare de l'Ouest, 154–55
Gare Montparnasse, xiii (map),
    155–64
    crash of 1895, 161–63, 164
    crash of 1900, 163
*Gare Montparnasse: The Melancholy
    of Departure* (de Chirico), 157, 158
Gauguin, Paul, 51, 56, 59, 63–71, 75
    Annah la Javanaïse, 69–71
    Self-Portrait, 68
    South Seas and, 65–71
    as Svengali look-alike, 63–64
Gault & Millau, 168–69
Gegenbach, Ernest de, 116–18
Gelenter, Terrance, 196–99
Genêt (Janet Flanner), 28–29
Genet, Jean, 149–50
Georges-Michel, Michel, 3, 114,
    134–35, 221
Gérôme, Jean-Léon, 80
Giacometti, Alberto, 44, 85
Gilbert, Jack, 149
Ginger Man, The (Donleavy), 150
Giovanni's Room (Baldwin), 195
Girodias, Maurice, 113, 147–50, 151
Glassco, John, 8, 37, 106
Goddard, Jacqueline, 4, 91–92

Gorgulov, Pavel, 112
La Goulue (The Glutton, Louise
    Weber), 19, 80
Gourat, Georges (Sem), 141
Graf, Christine, 195
Granowsky, Samuel, 113, 114
Grant, Cary, 129
Gray, Gilda, 137
Great Depression, 10–11
Great Gatsby, The (Fitzgerald), 123,
    125, 126
Gréco, Juliette, 160
Grieg, Edvard, 75
Grille d'Égout (Sewer Grating), 80
Grosz, George, 51
Le guide culinaire (Escoffier), 172

Hamnett, Nina, 89
Harrington, Curtis, 208
Harris, Frank, 34, 146, 197–99
hashish, 47, 146, 203
Hasty Bunch, A (McAlmon), 31
Haussmann, Georges-Eugène, 27,
    92, 154–55, 201
Hawes & Curtis, 131
Hazard (J.) grocery store, 37–38
H.D. (Hilda Doolittle), 31
Hébuterne, Jeanne, 54
Hemingway, Ernest
    anti-Semitism, 2–3
    apartment on rue du
        Cardinal-Lemoine, 8, 39–41
    and Bal de Printemps, 19–20
    and cafés, 4–8, 72–73, 125, 165
    "A Clean, Well-Lighted Place,"
        82
    concierge, 43–46

garret workroom at 39 rue Descartes, 73
To Have and Have Not, 122
housekeeper, 39–41
in our time, 3, 9, 31–32, 123
introduction to *Memoirs* (Kiki of Montparnasse), 36, 102
introduction to *Souvenirs* (Kiki of Montparnasse), 108
and "ladies of all sexes," 25
"Montparnasse," 6
as Montparno, 5–8, 111
A Moveable Feast, 1–4, 40–41, 124, 126–27
"My Life in the Bull Ring with Donald Ogden Stewart," 122, 124
and Ney statue, 80
and Le Sphinx, 186
and Donald Ogden Stewart, 120–22, 124–27
studio at 69 rue Froidevaux, xiii (map), 43–46
The Sun Also Rises, 19–20, 29–30, 33, 44, 120, 122, 125, 126
Three Stories and Ten Poems, 123
True at First Light, 43–45
and World War I, 111
Hemingway, Hadley (wife of Ernest), 19, 39–41, 43–44, 111, 128
Hemingway, John (Bumby, son of Ernest), 39, 40–41
Hemingway, Mary (wife of Ernest), 43
Hepburn, Katharine, 129
Herculaneum, 14

Herriot, Édouard, 183
Heysen, Hans, 57
Heysen, Nora, 57
Hiler, Hilaire (Hiler Harzberg), 216–17
Hodgkins, Frances, 52
Hoffenberg, Mason, 149
Hollywood Anti-Nazi League, 130–31
horseracing, 29–30
Hôtel Istria, 216, 222
hôtels de passe, 184–85
Hours Press, 30, 32
House of Mirth, The (Wharton), 111–12
House Un-American Activities Committee, 129–31
How to Be Happy on the Riviera, 166–67
Huddleston, Sisley, 28, 82–83, 195
Hugo, Victor, 21, 66
Hull, E. M., 62

Ideal Husband, An (Wilde), 199
Illness as Metaphor (Sontag), 208
impressionism, 56, 66–67
Inferno (Strindberg), 72
influenza epidemic (1918), 39
Ingres, Jean-Auguste-Dominique, 105
in our time (Hemingway), 3, 9, 31–32, 123
Isherwood, Christopher, 92

Jackson, Kevin, 206–13
Jacob, Max, 89
Janssonius, Johannes, 13

Jarry, Alfred, 206
java (dance), 134–35
Jazz Age, 137
Jesuits, 116–18
J. Hazard (grocery store), 37–38
Le Jockey, xiii (map), 216–23
    closing in 1930, 217
    Kiki of Montparnasse and,
        219–23
    naming, 217
    opening in 1923, 216–17
Jockey Club de Paris, 217
John, Gwen, 43
"JoJo le Terreur" (bodyguard), 189
Jolas, Eugene, 33
Joyce, James, 146
    "The Dead," 200
    Finnegan's Wake, 30, 33
    *Our Exagmination Round His
        Factification for Incamination of
        Work in Progress* (symposium
        on *Finnegan's Wake*), 30
    Ulysses, 31, 32, 145, 198
Judas, 200–201
Jules et Jim (Roché), 92–93

Kahane, Jack, 31, 145–47, 151–53
Karloff, Boris, 114
Kelly, Gene, 194–95
Kessel, Joseph, 188
Kharis ("The Fakir"), 113–14
Kiki of Montparnasse (Alice Prin),
    91, 92, 97–99, 100–101, 102–8
    at La Coupole, 107–8
    in *La galerie des monstres* (film),
        94, 222
    at Le Jockey, 219–23

Memoirs, 36, 95, 102
    Souvenirs, 104–5, 107–8
Kisling, Moïse, 89, 186
Koch, Howard, 24
Kremegne, Pinchus, 88
Krohg, Per, 75, 104, 216
Krohn, Hans von, 180–81

Ladoux, Georges, 180–81
Lady Chatterley's Lover (Lawrence), 36
Lafon, René, xix
Ländler (dance), 133–34
Last Nights of Paris (Soupault), 206
Last Tycoon, The (Fitzgerald),
    119–20
Latin Quarter, 5–6, 12–13
Lawrence, D. H., 34, 145
    The Escaped Cock, 32
    Lady Chatterley's Lover, 36
Ledoux, Claude Nicolas, 14–15
Left Bank, 168–69
Léger, Fernand, xxii, 89, 90
Légion d'Honneur, 183
Leigh, Vivien, 212–13
Lenin, Vladimir, 27–28, 59
L'exécution du maréchal Ney
    (Gérôme), 80
L'Herbier, Marcel, 222
Lhote, André, 56–57
Le lion des Mogols (film), 221–22
Lipchitz, Jacques, 89
little magazines, 33–36
Little Poems in Prose (Baudelaire), 36
Loeb, Harold, 33
Logue, Christopher, 149
Lolita (Nabokov), 113, 150
London Times, 28, 82–83

"lost generation" (Stein), 26
Louis XIV (France), 13
Louis XV (France), 17–18
Louvre, 48
"Love Song of J. Alfred Prufrock,
  The" (Eliot), xvii
Loy, Mina, 216
Lust (Logue), 149
Luxembourg Gardens, 46, 178

Macdonald, Ramsay, 128
Macron, Emmanuel, 1
Maddock, Lillian, 38–39
Maillol, Aristide, 68
Manet, Édouard, 59, 69–70
Man Ray, Juliet, 92, 205
Mardi Gras, 18
Mariette, Albert, 161–64
Mark Cross chain, 27
Martel, Charles, 189
Martin, Florence ("Flossie"), 110,
  222–23
Marx, Karl, 128
Massine, Léonid, 136–37
Mata Hari, 180–81
Mathieu press, 32
Matisse, Henri, 75
Maupassant, Guy de, 59
Maure, Thérèse (Thérèse Treize),
  216, 220
Mazarin, Cardinal-Duke Jules
  Raymond, 48
McAlmon, Robert, 30–31, 32–33,
  123–24, 217, 219
Melville, Herman, 9
Memoirs (Kiki of Montparnasse), 36,
  95, 102

Memoirs of Montparnasse (Glassco), 37
Mencken, H. L., 9
Menon, Ricardo, 203–5
Mesens, Édouard, 94, 97, 98
Miller, Henry, 7–8, 143, 145
  Anaïs Nin and, 147, 151
  Tropic of Cancer, 28–29, 146–47,
    148, 151–53
Miller, Lee, 98–99, 100
Les Misérables (Hugo), 21, 66
Miss Julie (Strindberg), 75
Mistinguett, 159
modèles de profession, 88–89. *See also*
  Kiki of Montparnasse (Alice
  Prin)
  Annah, 69–71
  art school, 49–50, 52, 54, 55–56
  Jacqueline Goddard, 4, 91–92
  Lee Miller, 98–99, 100
  Model Market, xiii (map), 58–60
Modigliani, Amedeo, xxi, 54, 56,
  59, 85, 89
Molard, Judith, 70
Molard, William, 70, 75
Le Monocle, 193
Montagnes Suisses (Swiss
  Mountains), 22
Montmartre, 58, 84, 104, 138, 201
Montparnasse, xiii (map)
  annexation by Paris (1725), 13
  cemetery (*See* Cimetière du
    Montparnasse)
  expatriate community, 1–11,
    24–36, 109–18
  high period (1920-1935), 10,
    24–26
  naming of, 12–13

Montparnasse (*cont.*)
    Paris absorbs (1669), 200
    social and racial tensions,
        xix–xx, 2–4
    as "the quarter," 1–6
    train station (*See* Gare Mont-
        parnasse)
    walls, 14–16, 73
    as *le zone*, 15
"Montparnasse" (Hemingway), 6
Montparnos, as term, 2–3, 5–6
Monts de Piété, 189
Moorhead, Ethel, 33–34
Moran, Lois, 222
Morgan, J. Pierpont, 27
morphine, 25
Mosjoukine, Ivan, 221–22
Moulin Rouge, 19, 80–81
Moveable Feast, A (Hemingway),
    1–4, 40–41, 124, 126–27
Mucha, Alphonse, 51–52, 56, 64, 65,
    67–68, 73
Mummy, The (film), 114
Munch, Edvard, 68, 75
Murphy, Gerald, 27, 44
musette de cour (bagpipe), 16–17
Musset, Alfred de, 1
My Life and Loves (Harris), 34, 198
*My Life as a Spy in the Service of
    France* (Richard), 181, 182
"My Life in the Bull Ring with
    Donald Ogden Stewart"
    (Hemingway), 122, 124

Nabokov, Vladimir, 113, 150
Napoleon Bonaparte, 79–80
Napoleonic Code, 183

Nazis, 159–60
Nevinson, C. R. W., 82–83
New Athens, 47
New Republic, The, 29–30
New Yorker, The, 28–29
Ney, Michel, 79–81
Ney, Michel (statue), xiii (map),
    72–75, 79–81
Nin, Anaïs, 145, 147, 151
1929 (almanac), 98
Ninotchka (film), 168
Noiret, Philippe, 203–5
Notebooks of Malte Laurids Brigge
    (Rilke), 85
Notes on Camp (Sontag), 206
Nusch, 93

Obelisk (Pearson), 145–47
Obelisk Press, 31, 145–47
Oberlé, Jean, 218–19
Olympia (Manet), 69–70
Olympia Press, 147–50
one-step (dance), 136–37
opium, 25, 47, 140, 146, 203
Oppenheim, Méret, 93
Orwell, George, 143
Ouida, 62
*Our Exagmination Round His
    Factification for Incamination of
    Work in Progress* (symposium on
    Finnegan's Wake), 30

Pack, Nina, 69
painting *en plein air*, 56
Parade (ballet), 136–37
Le Paradis, 159
Parc aux Cerfs (Deer Park), 17–18

Paris Herald, 28
Paris-Montparnasse (periodical), 95, 103–4, 107–8
Paris Times, 28
Parker, Robert B., 179
Parnassus, 12–13
Pascin, Jules, xxii, 48, 186, 217
Pearson, Neil, 143–47, 151–53
Pellerin, Guillaume-Marie, 161–64
Père Lachaise, 201
Péret, Benjamin, 28, 96–97, 117
Perkins, Maxwell, 123, 125–26
Perlès, Alfred, 146, 147
Le Pétomane, 19
Petrified Forest, The (Sherwood), 8–9
Pfeiffer, Pauline (wife of Ernest Hemingway), 41, 44, 46
Philadelphia Story, The (film), 129
Piaf, Édith, 183
Picabia, Francis, 48
Picasso, Pablo, xxi–xxii, 27, 113, 193–94
Pigeon, Charles, 201–2
pimping, 183
Pissarro, Camille, 66
Place Denfert-Rochereau, 14–15
Place de Rennes, 162–63
Plath, Sylvia, 154
Plaza de Toros (Pamplona), 121–23, 124
Poiret, Paul, 51
Pompidour, Madame de, 17–18
pornography. *See* erotica
Porter, Cole, 27
Poulenc, Francis, 136–37
Pound, Ezra, 35–36, 146–47

Powell, Michael, 29
Pressburger, Emeric, 29
Prévert, Jacques, 160, 186
Prin, Alice. *See* Kiki of Montparnasse (Alice Prin)
Prix de Rome, 50
Prohibition, 25
prostitution, 16, 19, 58–59, 102–3, 179–90
Proust, Marcel, 183
Putnam, Samuel, 108, 214–15

Rank, Otto, 151
Ranson, Paul, 57
Ravel, Maurice, 68
Ray, Man, 28, 29, 91–101, 186
    grave, 205
    home, xiii (map)
    models, 4, 91–92, 94, 98–101
        (*See also* Kiki of Montparnasse (Alice Prin))
    studios, xiii (map), 83–85, 95, 100–101, 216
    Le violin d'Ingres (Ray), 105
Redon, Odilon, 85
Renoir, Jean, 89
Le rêve transformé (*The Transformed Dream*) (de Chirico), 157
La revolution Surréalist (periodical), 116
Revue nègre, 137, 221
Rézard des Wouves, Jean, 157–58
Richard, Marthe, 179–85
Richer, Henry, 180
Richer, Marthe. *See* Richard, Marthe
Rilke, Rainer Maria, 85, 216
Rivera, Diego, 89

Robbe-Grillet, Alain, 209–10
Robia, Rosalie, 85, 86
Robiquet, Victor, xxii
Roché, Henri-Pierre, 92–93, 97
Rodin, Auguste, 174, 203, 216
Rohrbach, Marie, 39–41
roller skating, 78, 80–81
Root, Waverley, 32–33
Rosa la Rouge (Rosa the Red), 59
Rossi, Carmen, 52
Ross, Lillian, 4
La Rotonde, xiii (map), 1, 194
    dance floor, 138
    freeloaders, 7–8
    Hemingway and, 5
    opening in 1910, 4–5
    Spaniards and, 6
Rousseau, Henri ("Le Douanier"),
    15, 64–65
Rousseau, Jean-Jacques, 66
Rubinstein, Helena, 30
La Ruche, 87–90
La Ruche (Léger), 90
Rude, François, 79–81
rue Blomet, 157–60
rue Bréa, xiii (map), 21–23
rue Campagne-Première, 14, 83–85,
    100–101, 168, 216–23
rue de la Grande-Chaumière, 5,
    21–23, 48–60, 77, 82–83, 168
rue Delambre, xiii (map), 35–36, 84,
    110–11, 125–27
rue Descartes, 73
rue du Cardinal-Lemoine, 8, 39–41
rue Froidevaux, xiii (map), 43–46
rue Notre Dame des Champs, xiii
    (map)

rue Stanislas, xiii (map)
rue Vavin, xiii (map)
rue Vercingétorix, 67, 69–71
rumba (dance), 137
Ryall, Bill (William Bolitho), 208–9

Sade, Marquis de, 149
Saint-Germain-des-Prés, 159–60
Saint Phalle Niki de, 203–5
Salmon, André, xxi–xxii
Salon des Indépendants, 64
Salon des Refusés, 201
salt, 15
Santé, Luc, 62
Santé Prison, 193
Sartre, Jean-Paul, 89, 160, 186,
    193, 203
Satie, Erik, 136–37
sauce tartare, 172
School of Paris, 48
Seabrook, William, 93
Le Sélect, xiii (map), 9, 191–99
    opening in 1923, 4–5
    terrace, 196–99
Sem (Georges Gourat), 141
servants, 38–46
sexually transmitted diseases, 59,
    179, 184–85
sexual orientation, 25, 30–31, 187,
    193, 194, 198–99
Shahn, Ben, 129
Shakespeare and Company, 30–31,
    198
Shakespeare, William, 210, 212–13,
    214
Shaw, George Bernard, 132, 197
Sheik, The (film), 62

Sherwood, Robert, 8–9
shimmy (dance), 137
Simenon, Georges, 188
Simon, Arlette, 189
Simon, Lucien, 57
1601 (Twain), 33
Ślewiński, Władysław, 56
small presses, 30–33, 144–53, 198
Smith, Bill, 120
smoking. *See* tobacco
Sologne, Madeleine, 187
Sondheim, Stephen, 12
Sontag, Susan, 206–13
Soupault, Philippe, 206
Southern, Terry, 149
Soutine, Chaim, 48, 89, 104
Souvenirs (Kiki of Montparnasse),
    104–5, 107–8
Spanish Civil War, 130–31
Le Sphinx, xiii (map), 183, 186–90
Spirito François, 187–88, 189
Stavisky, Alexandre, 189
Stearns, Harold, 29–30, 196
Steffens, Lincoln, 128
Stein, Gertrude, 26, 27, 38, 126
Stewart, Donald Ogden, 119–31
    and Fitzgerald, 119–20, 123–27
    and Hemingway, 120–22, 124–27
Stewart, James, 129
stock market crash (1929), 10
Strachey, John, 130
Street, Julian, 5–6, 167–68
Strindberg, August, 68, 72, 73–77,
    125
Stroheim, Eric von, 181, 182
Studio in Montparnasse, A
    (Nevinson), 82–83

Sun Also Rises, The (Hemingway),
    19–20, 29–30, 33, 44, 120, 122,
    125, 126
Surrealism, 28, 32, 91–94, 96, 98,
    116–18, 157, 206
Svengali, 61–64
syphilis, 59, 179

tango (dance), 137, 138–42
Le Tango (undergarment), 139
Tango of the Archangel, The (van
    Dongen), 140–42
telephones, 4, 187
Tender is the Night (Fitzgerald), 222
This Quarter (periodical), 33–34,
    35–36
Thomas, Dylan, 201
Thomas, Madame Augustine, 139
Three Mountains Press, 31–32
Three Stories and Ten Poems
    (Hemingway), 123
Thurber, James, 209
Tickson, 21
Titus, Edward, 2–3, 30, 33, 35–36,
    108
tobacco, 25, 55, 62, 75, 134, 141, 157,
    175, 195, 218
To Have and Have Not
    (Hemingway), 122
Toklas, Alice B., 25, 38, 166
Toulouse-Lautrec, Henri de, 59, 75
Tour Maine-Montparnasse, 154–55
transition (periodical), 10, 33, 36
Tree, Herbert Beerbohm, 63
Treize, Thérèse (Thérèse Maure),
    216, 220
Trilby (du Maurier), 61–62

Trocchi, Alexander, 149
Tropic of Cancer (Miller), 28–29,
    146–47, 148, 151–53
Trotsky, Leon, 27–28
True at First Light (Hemingway), 43–45
tuberculosis, 26, 34, 59
Twain, Mark, 33
Tyler, Parker, 146
Tzara, Tristan, 28

Ulysses (Joyce), 31, 32, 145, 198
Utrillo, Maurice, 104

Valadon, Suzanne, 104
Valentino, Rudolph, 62, 138, 221–22
van Dongen, Kees, 48, 140–42,
    186–87
van Gogh, Vincent, 66–67, 68, 75
Vanity Fair (periodical), 122, 124
Variétiés (periodical), 95, 96
Vassilieff, Marie, xxii–xxiii, 103,
    111, 112–13
Venus, Brenda, 147
Verlaine, Paul, 73, 76
Versailles, 17–18, 163
Vian, Boris, 160
Vidal, George, 143–44
Le violin d'Ingres (Ray), 105
Vogue (periodical), 28
Voisin, 168

Vollard, Ambroise, 69
Volstead Act (1920), 25
Voltaire, 149
Vorobiev, Marevna, 54–55
Voronoff, Serge, 112–13

Wainhouse, Austryn, 149
Walsh, Ernest, 33
waltz, 133–34
Weber, Louise (La Goulue), 19, 80
Whale, James, 208
Wharton, Edith, 111–12
Where Paris Dines (Street), 167–68
Whistler, James McNeill, 52, 53,
    57, 85
Wilde, Oscar, 197, 198–99
Williams, William Carlos, 33
Wilson, Edmund, 120
Winter, Ella, 128–30
World War I, xxii–xxiii, 24–26,
    38–39, 82, 111, 135–37, 179
World War II, 157, 159–60, 180–90
Wyspiański, Stanisław, 59

Zadkine, Ossip, 52–54, 89
Zelle, Margaretha ("Mata Hari"),
    180–81
Zellweger, Renée, 143
"zinc," 3
Zola, Émile, 75–76

Photo by Rudy Gelenter

About the Author

JOHN BAXTER has lived in Paris for more than twenty years. He is the author of many critically acclaimed books about France, including *Montmartre: Paris's Village of Art and Sin*, *Saint-Germain-des-Prés: Paris's Rebel Quarter*, *Five Nights in Paris: After Dark in the City of Light*, *The Perfect Meal: In Search of the Lost Tastes of France* (winner of the IACP Cookbook Award for Culinary Travel), *The Most Beautiful Walk in the World: A Pedestrian in Paris*, *Immoveable Feast: Paris at the End of the World*, and *We'll Always Have Paris: Sex and Love in the City of Light*. Baxter, who gives literary walking tours through Paris, is also a film critic and biographer whose subjects have included the directors Federico Fellini, Stanley Kubrick, Woody Allen, and, most recently, Josef von Sternberg. Born in Australia, Baxter lives with his wife and daughter in the Saint-Germain-des-Prés neighborhood, in the building Sylvia Beach once called home.

www.johnbaxterparis.com

BOOKS BY JOHN BAXTER

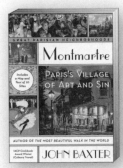

Great Parisian Neighborhoods
MONTMARTRE
Paris's Village of Art and Sin
Available in Paperback and E-Book

John Baxter leads us on a whirlwind tour of Montmartre, the hilltop village that fired the greatest achievements of modern art while also provoking bloody revolution and the sexual misbehavior that made Paris synonymous with sin.

**Great Parisian
Neighborhoods**
SAINT-GERMAIN-DES-PRÉS
Paris's Rebel Quarter
Available in Paperback and E-Book

A unique blend of history, memoir, and sightseeing essentials, as the award-winning chronicler of life in Paris reveals the secrets of his home quarter.

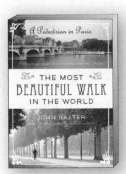

THE MOST BEAUTIFUL WALK IN THE WORLD
A Pedestrian in Paris
Available in Paperback and E-Book

NATIONAL BESTSELLER

Baxter reveals the most beautiful walks through Paris, including the favorite routes of artists and writers who have called the city home.

FIVE NIGHTS IN PARIS
After Dark in the City of Light
Available in Paperback and E-Book

John Baxter introduces you to the city's streets after dark, revealing hidden treasures and unexpected delights as he takes you through five of the city's greatest neighborhoods.

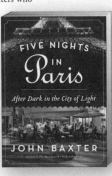

WE'LL ALWAYS HAVE PARIS
Sex and Love in the City of Light
Available in Paperback and E-Book

"A charming insider's guide to literary and artistic Paris. . . . Excellent." —*Daily Mail* (London)

THE PERFECT MEAL
Available in Paperback and E-Book
IACP COOKBOOK AWARD WINNER (*Culinary Travel*)

"Full of humor, insight, and mouth-watering details, *The Perfect Meal* is a delightful tour of 'traditional' French culture and cuisine." —*Travel + Leisure*

IMMOVEABLE FEAST
A Paris Christmas
Available in Paperback and E-Book

The charming, funny, and improbable tale of how a man who was raised on white bread—and didn't speak a word of French—ended up preparing the annual Christmas dinner for a venerable Parisian family.

PARIS AT THE END OF THE WORLD
The City of Light During the Great War, 1914-1918
Available in Paperback and E-Book

John Baxter brings to life one of the most dramatic and fascinating periods in Paris's history. As World War I ravaged France, the City of Light blazed more brightly than ever. Despite the terrifying sounds that could be heard from the capital, Parisians lived with urgency and without inhibition. The rich hosted wild parties, artists such as Picasso reached new heights, and the war brought a wave of foreigners, including Ernest Hemingway, to Paris for the first time. In this brilliant book, Baxter shows how the Great War forged the spirit of the city we love today.